Conversations with Emperor Jahangir

Bibliotheca Iranica
Literature Series No. 4

No. 1
Once a Dewdrop
Essays on the Poetry of Parvin E`tesami
Edited by Heshmat Moayyad

No. 2
Suppressed Persian
An Anthology of Forbidden Literature
Paul Sprachman

No.3
Reading Nasta`liq
Persian and Urdue Hands from 1500 to the Present
William L. Hanaway and Brain Spooner

No. 5
Welcoming Fighānī
Imitation and Poetic Individuality in
the Safavid-Mughal *Ghazal*
Paul E. Losensky

Conversations With Emperor Jahangir

by

"Mutribi" al-Asamm Samarqandi

Translated from the Persian with an Introduction by

Richard C. Foltz

MAZDA PUBLISHERS
1998

Mazda Publishers
Academic Publishers Since 1980
P.O. Box 2603
Costa Mesa, California 92626 U.S.A.
www.mazdapub.com

Library of Congress Cataloging-in-Publication Data
Muṭribī al-Aṣamm al-Samarqandī, b. 1559
[Khātimah. English]
Conversations with Emperor Jahangir/ by Mutribi al-Asamm
Samarqandi; translated with an introduction by Richard Foltz.
p.cm.—(Bibliotheca Iranica: Literature series; No. 4)
Includes bibliographical references and index.

ISBN:1-56859-069-5
(pbk.:alk. paper)

1. Jahangir, Emperor of Hindustan, 1569-1627. 2. India—Emperors—
Biography. 3. Muṭribī al-Aṣamm al-Samarqandī, b. 1559. 4. India—
Courts and courtiers—Biography. I. Title. II. Series.
DS461.5.M8313 1998
954.02'56'092—dc21
[B]
98-9901
CIP

To my father-in-law, Dr. Ali Navab

Contents

Acknowledgements

I first read Mutribi's text as a graduate student at Harvard with Ahmad Mahdavi-Damghani. I am grateful to Stephen Dale, Ruth Foltz, Robert McChesney, Ali Navab, and Annemarie Schimmel who read the translation and offered their comments, to Walter Feldman for his comments on chapter 15, and to Kemal Abdel-Malek for suggestions on the Arabic passages. I alone, however, am responsible for any errors.

Most of all, I would like to thank my beloved wife, Désirée, for her constant love, support and inspiration, and for our beautiful daughter Shahrzad.

Introduction

The present work is an account by a poet and scholar from Samarqand of his audiences with the Mughal Emperor of India, Jahangir, during a two-month period in 1627, the last year of Jahangir's life. The Central Asian visitor, who has not been identified from any contemporary sources, is known only by his pen-name, Mutribi, "the minstrel", which he apparently earned for his talents as a musician, and the epithets "al-Haqqi" ("divine truth") and "al-Asamm" ("the deaf one")[1]. The only other clues to his identity are his statements that he is descended from Malik Arghun on his father's side and the poet Basiri[2] on his mother's. His work has exceptional value as an historical document, and his intimate style is an exceedingly rare example for its place and time.

The work is comprised largely of verbatim accounts of the author's personal conversations with the Emperor, accompanied by his own commentary and relevant anecdotes and verses which he inserts. Like any would-be scholar of his age, Mutribi presents himself as a renaissance man with a strong foundation in Islamic religious scholarship, great poetic skill and the ability to compose extemporaneous verses appropriate to any occasion, as well as a thorough knowledge of the whole Persian poetic tradition. The Emperor Jahangir, too, sees himself as possessing all these gentlemanly abilities and interests.

---

[1] It is also an epithet for the month of Rajab.
[2] See pages 56 and 83.

Jahangir's own personal memoirs, published as the *Tuzuk-i Jahangiri* or *Jahangir-nama* (Book of Jahangir)[3], are, in the tradition of the autobiographical *Babur-nama*[4] written by his great grandfather who founded the Mughal dynasty in India, themselves an unusually frank and intimate account of the courtly life of the time. Mutribi's work offers a happy complement to the memoirs of Jahangir, both because Mutribi describes the end of the Emperor's reign, after the *Tuzuk* leaves off, and because the visitor's plebian perspective is so different from that of the Emperor. Mutribi provides many fascinating details about the Mughal court, as well as lifestyles, attitudes, and personal interactions of the time, which are not to be found in any other type of contemporary document.

Finally, this work offers strong evidence of the cultural connections which were maintained between Central and South Asia during the Mughal period, and as such, a corrective to the standard division applied in modern times to these cultural spheres which in many ways were not two but one.[5] The Mughals themselves were of Central Asian origin, and never forgot their roots as descendants of the fourteenth century conqueror Timur-i Lang ("Timur the Lame"), known in the West as Tamerlane. The Mughal rulers ensured a continuous flow of Central Asian influence into India throughout the sixteenth and seventeenth centuries by encouraging visitors and immigration.

The informal style of Mutribi's account and the very fact that such a personal document survived is highly unusual, but his experience was anything but uncommon. Scores of Central Asian immigrants mentioned in Mughal sources no doubt had

---

[3]The English translation is by Alexander Rogers and Henry Beveridge, published in Calcutta in 1909-14 and reprinted several times in India and Pakistan. A new English translation by Wheeler Thackston, Jr. is due to appear in 1998.

[4]Wheeler M. Thackston, Jr., tr., *The Baburnama*, Washington: Smithsonian and New York: Oxford University Press, 1996.

[5]See my *Mughal India and Central Asia*, Karachi: Oxford University Press, 1998; especially the Introduction.

very similar experiences, and one can only imagine there must have been hundreds more who remain anonymous.[6]

Mutribi's life

Our author states that he was seventy years of age when he came to Jahangir's court in 1627. This would put his birth in about 1559, or 966 of the Arabic lunar calendar. He appears to have had a traditional Islamic education as a child in Samarqand, and some musical training as well, before setting off for Bukhara to further his education there. In Bukhara he became a student of the well-known Naqshbandi sufi master Hasan Nisari[7], from whom he learned the canon of Persian poets and poetry of the time. He also continued his musical studies, refining his skills on the *nay* and the *qanun* under Kamal al-Din Hafiz 'Abd al-Rahim.[8] He later studied music under Yawmi Balkhi, philosophy under Yusuf Qarabaghi, theology under Nizari Badakhshi, book illumination under Rustam Naqqash, and calligraphy under Sabit Miankali.[9]

Mutribi claims in one of his works to have known such Shibanid rulers as 'Abdullah Khan II[10], 'Abd al-Mu'min Khan[11],

---

[6]Another Central Asian travelogue, which dates from the same period as Mutribi's, is that of Mahmud bin Amir Vali of Balkh. I have compared and contrasted these two travelogues in "Two 17th Century Central Asian Travellers to Mughal India," *Journal of the Royal Asiatic Society*, 3rd series, 6/3 (1996), 367-377, and intend to prepare an English edition of Mahmud's account in the near future.

[7]d. 1605.

[8]'Abd al-Ghani Mirzoev, *Khatirat-i Mutribi*, Karachi: Institute of Central and West Asian Studies, 1977, 3.

[9]B.A. Ahmedov, "Tazkira Mutribi kak istochnik po istorii i kul'ture xvi-xvii vv," *Istochnikovedenie i tekstologiia*, Moscow: Nauka, 1984, 38.

[10]r. 1583-1598.

[11]r. 1598-1599.

and princes such as Abdal Sultan[12] Bahadur Sultan[13], Abu'l-Khayr Sultan and Muzaffar Sultan[14] personally, and may have been in the service of some of them. It appears at least that he was in the service of the Samarqand governor Javanmard 'Ali Khan during the 1570s, and from 1585 that of Hajji Biy Kushchi.[15] Eventually he obtained the patronage of the Ashtarkhanid ruler Vali Muhammad Khan[16], which would appear not to have been until Mutribi was in his forties. When his patron died in 1612 Mutribi decided to start planning a trip to India, apparently more out of hope of enjoying the financial rewards of the Mughal emperor than out of any interest in travel or seeing foreign lands. His personal finances seem to have been precarious following Vali Muhammad's death, since Mutribi states that because of his responsibility of providing for twenty family members it took him nearly ten years before he was able to make arrangements to leave for India.

Mutribi's plan was to revise an anthology of poets which he had written for Vali Muhammad and offer it to the Mughal Emperor in hopes of thereby winning royal favor and material gain. With this in mind he set out for Balkh and Badakhshan in 1622 in order to do further research on Central Asian Persophone poets. He interviewed living poets in Balkh, Talighan, Fayzabad, Qunduz and elsewhere during this trip.[17] He then spent most of 1624 working the new information into his anthology, and in

---

[12]a.k.a. 'Abd al-Malik Sultan, son of the Shibanid ruler 'Abd al-Latif (r. 1540-1552); he was for a time governor of Samarqand.

[13]son of the Shibanid prince Sultan Sa'id Khan, and grandson of Abu Sa'id (r. 1530-33).

[14]They were sons of Samarqand governor Javanmard 'Ali Khan (r. 1572-1578), who was also a son of Abu Sa'id.

[15]*Tazkira al-Shu'ara*, Institute of Oriental Studies, Uzbekistan Academy of Sciences, MS no. 2253, ff. 4b-22b; see Ahmedov, "Tazkira Mutribi", 37.

[16]r. 1604-1611.

[17]Mirzoev, *Khatirat*, 4.

early 1625, accompanied by his son Muhammad 'Ali, he set out for India.

During stops in Balkh and Kabul Mutribi gathered further information, so that when he finally arrived at Lahore in 1626 he spent a month further revising his anthology before presenting himself at court. After all this work, Mutribi was clearly disappointed by the scant interest Emperor Jahangir initially showed in the anthology. The Emperor was far more interested in talking about Central Asia, grilling Mutribi with questions about famous figures there and other subjects. All the Mughal emperors were keenly aware of their Central Asian roots and Timurid lineage, and Jahangir felt a particularly intense attachment for his ancestral lands which his own son Shah Jahan would later work so hard to recapture.[18] The Emperor does eventually get around to having Mutribi's book read to him, and is sufficiently impressed to ask his visitor to incorporate an anthology of his own into Mutribi's work.

In all Mutribi spent only two months at the Court of Lahore, before begging leave to return home to Samarqand. The Emperor released Mutribi on the condition that he return to India within a year, but as Jahangir himself was to pass away within the following months and Mutribi was over seventy at that point, it appears most unlikely that second trip was ever made. In any event nothing further is heard of Mutribi, and it can be assumed he did not long survive his royal host.

Mutribi's works

Two works bearing Mutribi's name are known to us. The first is the anthology of poets which he composed for his patron Vali Muhammad Khan in 1604, entitled simply *Anthology of Poets*. This work exists in manuscript form in the library of the Oriental Institute of the Uzbekistan Academy of Sciences[19], and is written in imitation of the style of his teacher Hasan Nisari's

---

[18]See my, "The Mughal Occupation of Balkh, 1646-7," *Journal of Islamic Studies* 7/1 (1996), 49-61.

[19]*Tazkira al-Shu'ara*, MS no. 2253.

more famous work *Remembrance of Friends*[20]. Mutribi's first anthology mentions 320 Central Asian, Iranian and Indian poets of the time.

Mutribi later revised and re-focused this work with the intention of offering it as a gift to Emperor Jahangir, as discussed above. In this second anthology Mutribi deletes mention of Central Asian poets except those who went to work in India. The second anthology mentions only 292 poets in all. The only known manuscript exists in the India Office Library in London, where it was miscatalogued by Hermann Ethé under the title *Tarikh-i Jahangiri* (History of Jahangir)[21], under which name it also appears in Charles Storey's *Persian Literature*[22].

The later manuscript consists of three components. The first is Mutribi's revised anthology, which he refers to as *Nuskha-yi Ziba-yi Jahangiri* (The Beautiful Book of Jahangir). Attached to the anthology is a postscript (*khatima*), which is Mutribi's personal account of his audiences with the Emperor. This is the present work. A printed Persian edition of this second section was prepared by the late Tajik scholar 'Abd al-Ghani Mirzoev.[23] It is not a critical edition, however. Mirzoev provides almost no references for citations within the text, and his transcription contains numerous errors. Finally, there is a short anthology compiled by Jahangir in 1593-94 of eighty-one poets of his father Akbar's reign, which Mutribi incorporated into his own anthology at the Emperor's request. Mirzoev published a printed version of this section in Pakistan in 1976.[24]

---

[20]*Muzakkir-i Ahbab*, Hyderabad, Pakistan, 1969. An Uzbek version was published in Tashkent in 1993.

[21]Hermann Ethé, *Catalogue of Persian Manuscripts in the India Office Library*, Oxford, 1937, ii, 10-11, MS no. 3023.

[22]Charles Storey, *Persian Literature: A Bio-Bibliographical Survey*, London: Luzac & Co., 1927- , vol. i, pt. 2, 814, no. 1118.

[23]Mirzoev, *Khatirat*.

[24]'Abd al-Ghani Mirzoev, ed., *Nuskha-yi Ziba-yi Jahangiri*, Karachi: Institute of Central and West Asian Studies, 1976.

Thus Mutribi's literary contribution appears to consist in its essence of an anthology of poets who wrote in Persian, which he revised so that it exists in two distinct versions twenty-three years apart, the latter of which includes the account of his stay in Lahore which I have translated here. I am not aware of any other works by this author, or of any mention of him in contemporary sources. Since we know him only by his pen-name, however, it is not impossible that he appears elsewhere under some other nomenclature.

The Mughals and Central Asia

Zahir al-Din Muhammad Babur, who established the Mughal Empire in India following his victory over Ibrahim Lodi at the Battle of Panipat in 1526, was a fifth-generation descendant of the fourteenth century Central Asian Turkish conqueror Amir Timur Gurgan (Tamerlane). Babur was born in Andijan in the Ferghana valley of what is now the Republic of Uzbekistan. Following the model of his illustrious ancestor he himself managed to rule from Samarqand briefly on two occasions. The Timurid heyday of the fifteenth century had drawn to a close, however, and nomadic armies led by the Uzbek Shibani Khan prevented Babur from holding onto his ancestral possessions in Transoxiana. For years Babur ruled an exile kingdom from his capital at Kabul, occasionally leading raids into India until he finally relocated there following his victory at Panipat. Babur was no lover of India, however, as the following passage from his memoirs illustrates:

> Hindustan is a place of little charm. There is no beauty in its people, no graceful social intercourse, no poetic talent or understanding, no etiquette, no nobility or manliness. In the arts and crafts there is no harmony or symmetry, there are no good horses, no good meat, no good grapes, melons or fruit. There is no ice, no cold water, no good food or bread in the

markets. There are no baths and no *madrasa*s. There
are no candles, torches, or candlesticks.[25]

Babur pined for the fountains, the melons, and the air of the
Central Asian home he was never again to see. "How can one
forget the pleasures of that country," he writes in a letter to his
sufi master in Samarqand; "...how can one forget a licit pleasure
like melons and grapes?"[26] His nostalgia set the tone for his
successors, who went on to build in India the largest, wealthiest
empire of the time but never ceased to speak and think of Central Asia with longing. Babur's son Humayun would have led his
armies to a reconquest of Samarqand had his brother Kamran
not mutinied in 1549 near Balkh.[27]

Akbar, under whose enlightened rule northern India flour-
ished throughout the second half of the sixteenth century, had
similar ambitions. The official chronicle of his reign, the *Akbar-
nama*, states that "Should the wide country of India be civilized
by means of obedient vassals he (Akbar) would proceed to
Turan... In this way the various classes of mankind would experience the joys of concord".[28] In 1587 Akbar's court chronicler
Abu'l Fazl writes that at last "His Majesty has turned his attention to the conquest of Turan."[29] In fact Akbar never did so,
since at that time the Uzbeks were enjoying a period of exceptional strength and stability under 'Abdullah Khan.

Mutribi's Indian host Emperor Jahangir strongly maintains
the mindset of his forebears regarding Central Asia. As he says
in his own memoirs, the *Tuzuk-i Jahangiri*:

---

[25]Thackston, *Babur-nama*, 350.

[26]Thackston, *Babur-nama*, 423.

[27]Gulbadan Begum, *Humayun-nama*, tr. Annette S. Beveridge,
London: Royal Asiatic Society, 1902 (reprint Lahore, 1987), 188.

[28]Abu'l Fazl 'Allami, *Akbar-nama*, tr. H. Beveridge, 3 vols., Calcutta:
Royal Asiatic Society of Bengal, 1902-1939, iii, 616-7.

[29]Riazul Islam, *A Calendar of Documents on Indo-Persian Relations*,
v.2, Tehran, 1982, 207.

My intention... was of two kinds; one, that inasmuch as the conquest of Transoxiana was always in the pure mind of my revered father, though every time he determined on it things occurred to prevent it, if this business [of getting Hindu rulers to submit] could be settled, and this danger dismissed from my mind, I would leave [my son] Parviz in Hindustan, and in reliance on Allah, myself start for my hereditary territories...[30]

And later:

As I had made up my exalted mind to the conquest of Transoxiana, which was the hereditary kingdom of my ancestors, I desired to free the face of Hindustan from the rubbish of the factious and rebellious, and leaving one of my sons in that country, to go myself with a valiant army in due array, with elephants of mountainous dignity and of lightening speed, and taking ample treasure with me, to undertake the conquest of my ancestral dominions.[31]

Mutribi's account of his conversations with Jahangir gives ample evidence, if any were needed, corroborating the Emperor's intense interest and preoccupation with Central Asia, specifically the state of his ancestor Timur's tomb, and information regarding important Central Asian religious and political figures. Indeed this is perhaps the major theme of the work, and as such it provides an illustration of this aspect of the Emperor's personality which is unparalleled in its richness and detail, even by comparison with Jahangir's own memoirs.

Emperor Jahangir's Life and Character

In a real sense the principal subject of Mutribi's account is the Emperor Jahangir himself. Jahangir's biography is readily ac-

---

[30]*Tuzuk-i Jahangiri*, i, 26.

[31]*Tuzuk-i Jahangiri*, i, 89.

cessible from numerous sources[32], but a short summary will be given here. He was born at the village of Sikri near Agra on the seventeenth of the month of Rabi' al-awwal, 977 of the Hijri calendar, or August thirty-first, 1569, after the Chishti sufi saint Shaykh Salim had foretold his birth to Akbar.[33] The infant prince was named Salim in honor of this shaykh, and in fulfillment of a vow Akbar built a new city on that site which became the Mughal capital of Fatehpur Sikri for fourteen years.

When Salim acceded to the throne on October twenty-fourth, 1605 (20 Jumada al-thani 1014 A.H.), he decided to take a new name since Salim was also the name of the Ottoman Emperor. "An inspiration from the hidden world," he writes in his memoirs, "brought it into my mind that, inasmuch as the business of kings is the controlling of the world, I should give myself the name of Jahangir ("World-seizer") and make my title of honor Nur al-Din ("Light of the Faith"), inasmuch as my sitting on the throne coincided with then rising and shining on the earth of [the Sun]".[34]

Jahangir initially seems to have been supported by a faction of religious scholars and sufi shaykhs who had opposed his father Akbar's heterodox policies, but he was no religious zealot, and he actually imprisoned the revivalist sufi master Ahmad Sirhindi for "insubordination". In the event Jahangir maintained to a large extent his father's ecumenical interests, though not to such an extreme. Europeans, who had been present at Akbar's court, became increasingly visible, as did European influence and iconography in Jahangir period painting.

His reign was threatened by rebellions on several occasions. The first was by his son Khusraw in 1606. He lost the stategic northwestern city of Qandahar to the Iranian Safavids in 1622. In 1624 another son, Khurram, who was to succeed him as Shah

---

[32]See, for example, the biography *Jahangir* by Muni Lal (Delhi: Vikas, 1983); also Beni Prasad, *History of Jahangir*, Allahabad: Indian Press, 1940.

[33]*Tuzuk*, i, 2.

[34]*Tuzuk*, i, 2-3.

Jahan, rebelled in the south. Finally in 1626 came the rebellion of his general Mahabat Khan, during which the Emperor was for a time taken prisoner by the rebel forces.

During much of his reign Jahangir was greatly influenced by his Persian wife Nur Jahan, whose father, brother, and other relatives obtained important administrative positions. Many historians have suggested it was Nur Jahan who held the actual reins of power, although her role continues to be debated.[35]

Jahangir struggled with alcohol and opium addiction throughout his life, which considerably weakened his consitution. He died on October twenty-seventh, 1627 (27 Safar 1057), on the way back to Lahore from his summer retreat in Kashmir, just months after Mutribi's visit.

The fourth emperor of the Mughal dynasty was, like his father Akbar and his great-grandfather Babur, a complex man of mixed qualities which ranged between extremes. He was a genuinely cultivated individual with a great appreciation for poetry and other refinements. He loved art and was a lavish patron with an active atelier of artists from Iran, Central Asia, and India. He had a keen sense of justice and of his own immense responsibility as ruler of a vast and heterogeneous empire. His memoirs, though not matching Babur's in candor and insight, at least approach them in those qualities. Like Babur he enjoyed a good time, and he goes into some detail about his drinking habits[36], and like Babur he considered himself a poet. "As I have a poetic disposition," he states in his memoirs, "I sometimes intentionally and sometimes involuntarily compose couplets and quatrains."[37] It appears in fact that at least in some sense he consciously modeled his memoirs on those of Babur. At one point he remarks that while Babur describes wildlife in his book, he never had it painted. Jahangir goes on to say that he has

---

[35]See the recent biography by Findly Ellison Banks, *Nur Jahan*, New York: Oxford University Press, 1996; also Chandra Pant, *Nur Jahan and Her Family*, Allahabad: Dandewal, 1978, and Prasad, *History*, 147-172.

[36]*Tuzuk*, i, 8.

[37]*Tuzuk*, i, 228.

commissioned illustrations of animals which he mentions in the *Tuzuk*.[38] Jahangir was also capable of what would appear by present-day standards to be horrifying and excessive cruelty. One example to be found in his memoirs where he describes a hunting expedition. The Emperor had just set his aim on a *nilgai*, when three attendants emerged unexpectedly from the bush and frightened the animal off. Jahangir had one of the offenders executed on the spot, and the other two crippled by having their heel tendons cut, then had them paraded around the camp on donkeys, "so that no one again should have the boldness to do such a thing."[39]

The Context of Mutribi's Encounters with the Emperor

Mutribi's dialogues with Jahangir take place in the context of royal assemblies (*majalis*), usually held in the evening, where the Emperor's attendants, advisors, and companions would gather in his company for discussions and often drinking and various forms of entertainment. Such gatherings were highly formalized, and where one was seated was an indication to all present of both rank and favor.[40] Most of the other attendees mentioned by Mutribi are known from other sources, and some are quite famous Mughal officials. Mutribi's account is one of the most—perhaps *the* most—vivid such description of royal Mughal assemblies in existence. He brings these events and the interactions of their participants to life in a way which is most rare in pre-modern sources for Mughal history; this is one of the major contributions of his work for the cultural historian.

---

[38]Tuzuk, i, 215.

[39]*Tuzuk*, i, 164.

[40]See the descriptions and visual depictions in Milo Cleveland Beach and Ebba Koch, *King of the World: The Padshahnama*, London: Azimuth, 1997, especially pp. 35-36, 92-97, and 133-134 which deal with Jahangir's period.

Persian Literature in Central Asia and India

That the literary works of Mutribi, a Central Asian from Samarqand, should fall under the rubric of Persian literature ought to come as no surprise to anyone familiar with the cultural history of Muslims in Central and South Asia. Although Samarqand is today the second city and former capital of an ostensibly Turkic-speaking republic, Uzbekistan, it was and remains a significant pole of the Persian cultural world. Even now the majority of the population speaks the Tajik dialect of Persian as its first language, and Persian is still the vehicle of choice for modern Samarqandi poets.[41]

Of course, the Mughals were ethnically a Turkic dynasty, just as most of the previous Muslim dynasties of northern India had been. But ever since the Turkic steppe peoples had first begun to embrace Islam in large numbers around the time of the Ghaznavids and Seljuks during the eleventh century, it was the Persian variant of Islamic civilization they encountered and embraced, inevitably becoming its champions and patrons. Like other Turkic rulers, the Mughals knew and continued to speak Turkish privately[42], but were fluent in Persian as well, and it was the latter language they patronized and employed in their administrations.

In fact Persian remained the administrative language of much of India even under the British, who officially replaced it with "Hindustani" or Urdu only during the mid-nineteenth century. Even today in South Asia among the older generation it is common to find educated people—Hindu as well as Muslim—who know Persian.

Many Iranians may be unaware that the corpus of Persian literature produced over the centuries in India actually far outweighs the amount produced in Iran proper during the same pe-

---

[41] See the recent anthology, *Guldasta-yi Samarqand*, Tashkent: Ghafur Ghulam and Dushanbe: Adib, 1989.

[42] Jahangir states in memoirs, "Notwithstanding that I grew up in Hindustan, I am not ignorant of Turki speech and writing" (*Tuzuk*, i, 109-110).

riod of time. In part this is due to the constant flow of skilled Iranian men of letters who migrated to India in search of more generous patrons than they found at home.[43] Mutribi's discussions of poets from Iran, Central Asia and India, all writing in Persian, demonstrates how far beyond the borders of Iran the influence of Persian literature was felt, and his book is itself a testament to the importance and vitality of the Persian language in Central and Southern Asia during the pre-modern period.

---

[43]See Ahmad Gulchin-Ma'ani, *Karvan-i Hind*, 2 vols., Mashhad: Astan-i Quds-i Razavi, 1370 (1990-91).

Prologue

In the name of Allah[44], *the Compassionate, the Merciful*
Allah is Great

The praise of the Omnipresent on high be upon the Master of the
Banner of Praise and the Blessed State [i.e., the Prophet]; Allah's peace be upon him and his family and his companions, and
witness their virtue; may the Paradise of Almighty Allah be
given to all Muslims.

It is well known that the Layer of the Foundations of Religious Law and the Bright Nation (peace, blessings greetings and
salutations be upon him) said, "Faith is twofold: half patience
and half gratitude."[45] That is to say, complete faith—which is
humanity's noblest state—is comprised of two attributes; one is
gratitude, and the other is patience. So the person with perfect
faith is the one who adorns his being with these two qualities,
gratitude in times of blessing and patience in times of trouble.

Gratitude in times of blessing means that when one is
blessed it is incumbent upon a believer to give thanks. And what
blessing could be greater than attendance at the heavenly court
of the mighty sultans? What vast benefits and innumerable sen-
timents result from a poor man's attendance on kings! Proximity
to kings is the best way to serve the needs of the people, and
especially attendance at the threshold of the throne of the King
of the kings of the lands of India, possessor of all that is most
glorious in the world, Hero of the Age and Subduer of the Op-
pressors of the Time, Steward of Grace and Dispenser of Royal

---

[44] The more generic terms *elahi* and *khuda* I have translated as "God"
where they occur in the text. "Allah" I have left untranslated.

[45] Ar. *Al-iman nisfan; nisf sabr wa nisf shukr.*

Favor, Protector of the Beneficent Realm, upon whom all creation relies, Valiant Lion of the Jungle and Holy Warrior of the
Light of the Nation and the World and the Faith, Emperor Jahangir son of Emperor Jalal al-Din Muhammad Akbar Ghazi,
Almighty Allah perpetuate his realm and his reign and support
his justice and his charity.

How well that master of hearts put it who brought the lip of
literacy to the high threshold of this Reflection of the Creator,
what thanks are incumbent on such supplicants:

> "What could be produced by hand or tongue
> That would be capable of expressing the thanks that are due?"
> [Sa'di]

Praise be to Allah, may He bless and exalt this great wealth
and the magnificent gifts of the territory of the joyous realm of
Lahore, Allah protect it from faults and weakness through the
stewardship of that Offspring of Wisdom, Repository of Quality
and Quantity Khwaja Fakhr al-Din Husayn[46], son of that master
of speech Mawlana Khwaja Khan-i Divan, Allah's peace be
upon him, to whom fell the lot of this poor, insignificant old
man. On Wednesday, the nineteenth of the month of Rabi' al-
Avval in the year 1036, two hours into the third watch[47], the
gaze of this diseased eye saw the Light of the Poets, this Noble
Shadow of Nourishment.[48]

> Thanks be to God that the eye, from your face, found il-
> lumination
> The heart, circumambulating the *ka'ba* of where you are,
> found presence
> The soul, from your lips, heard the tune called "Your
> Breath is in It"

---

[46]The governor of Lahore.

[47]Lit., "after two watches (*pahr*) and five *ghari*s." A *ghari* is 22 and a
half minutes.

[48]That is, he met the governor.

This seedling of a soul, from the breath of your ruby lips,
found form
Longing for servitude at your threshold
Mutribi found everything in this command.

How can one give thanks for this opportunity, and string the pearls of praise for this good fortune? However much happiness it enjoys, the mind is incapable of this; but, fortunately, this praise-giver has been able to benefit from the praise-givers of days gone by. Thus on Thursday, the ninth of Jumada al-Thani, 1036, dreams began to be realized. And trust is in Allah the Beloved.

First Meeting: Receiving Royal Gifts

Once the duties of honorable greetings and exaltations for this Reflection of the Creator and Arbiter over the Needs of the People had been carried out, his tongue of pearls asked of this incompetent narrator,

"How many days is it since you entered the joyous realm of Lahore?"

"One month," I said.

"So where have you been that it took you so long to come and pay our respects?" he asked.

"I have been writing *The Beautiful Book of Jahangir* to offer you as a present," I said. "That has kept me busy."

"What was the date of its completion?" he asked me. I offered him this quatrain by way of reply:

> "In the name of the world-turning Emperor Jahangir
> This pleasant work came to the pen
> Its meticulous author made the date of its completion
> Signified by *'The Beautiful Book of Jahangir'*"[49]

This being pleasing to His Enlightened Majesty, the high command was nobly conveyed: "Recite that again!"

---

[49] *Nuskha-yi Ziba-yi Jahangiri.* The numerical value (*abjad*) of this title equals 1035 A.H. (1625 C.E.). In Muslim court culture the ability to compose extemporaneous verse in response to any topic of conversation was considered a sign of great skill and intelligence, as was the ability to compose chronograms. Mutribi is attempting here to depict himself as a master of both.

And it was repeated. Then he asked me, "Are you planning to stay in this country, or will you return to your own country, or are you on your way to Mecca?"[50]

I replied, "O Qibla of the World, I will do whatever the Divine Viceregent commands. If he tells me to stay I will stay; if he tells me to go I will go; and if he sets out for the Blessed House, I will follow in his steps. Whatever fate has chosen for me, I leave the choice to His Majesty and am seeking only to do his will!" And I recited the following couplet:

"For anyone who is plagued by love
His beloved's will, is his will."

Then he said, "We are going to give you four presents. But not all at once, all right? The first is spending money[51], the second is clothing, the third is a riding horse, and the fourth is a slave-boy to serve you. Today which one would you like?"

In reply I recited the following couplet:

"Don't be without cash[52], for cash begets cash
Everyone gives credit to those who have cash
Some say credit is better than cash
But don't listen to him who puts credit above cash."

Immediately a plate full of rupees was brought in. There were a thousand rupees there, and each rupee is worth two and a half *misqal*s in Turanian money. And to this, that Agent of Divine Generosity Nur Jahan Begum—may her chastity be preserved—added the sum of five hundred rupees by way of her slave-girls. I responded with the following couplet:

---

[50]Due to political tensions with the Safavid rulers of Iran, who had made Shi'ism the state religion beginning in 1501, Central Asian Muslims generally travelled to the Hijaz via India. An alternate route was to the north of the Caspian and down through Ottoman territory.

[51]It was common practice for the Mughal emperors to cover the living expenses of ambassadors and other foreign visitors at court.

[52]lit., gold.

"By God, so long as the world exists may the King be Lord of the Auspicious Conjunction[53]
And Nur Jahan (lit., "The Light of the World) remain in the shadow of the King."

You might say this incident was similar to the time when Khwaja Shams al-Din Muhammad Hafiz of Shiraz waited on His Majesty Timur. The similarity lies in this, that according to Khwaja Hasan Nisari, when Amir Timur Gurgan conquered Shiraz, he called Khwaja Hafiz to come before him because of a concern he had in his regard. And the reason for this concern is a well-known story which is mentioned in most books, that when Hafiz came before him Timur said, "Ha! Hafiz! Don't you know that I have wielded my sword and conquered the world in order to build up Samarqand and Bukhara? Yet you would spoil my efforts by exchanging Samarqand and Bukhara for a Hindu mole! You said,

> 'If that Shirazi beauty (lit., "Turk") would just take my heart in hand
> For his/her black beauty-mark (lit., "Hindu mole") I'd trade Bukhara and Samarqand.'"

Since Khwaja Hafiz had by then become indigent and helpless he replied,
"Indeed, it is because of just this exchange that I have fallen into such a beggarly state."
His Majesty Timur found this reply amusing, and said,
"Hafiz, I'm going to make you a gift of four things, but I'm going to think of them secretly and not give them all at once, although they'll be appropriate to your needs. Since they call you 'the Mystic Tongue'[54], I'm going to test you and see if you can guess what my gifts are. Each one you guess, you'll get from me; whatever you don't guess, you won't get."

---

[53]*Sahib-qirani*, a title of Timur, which the Mughal emperors frequently took upon themselves in testimony to their Timurid lineage.
[54]Ar. *al-lisan al-ghayb*.

Hafiz extemporaneously recited,

> "O King, who has set the turban upon my head
> And protected me with his golden robe
> A bowl beneath a robe is an empty bag
> Kindly toss me a fistful of gold to fill it."

Timur said, "You've earned yourself clothing, but not a horse or saddle."

Hafiz replied, "Should you offer gold, a horse and saddle can be found in the bazaar."

Timur answered in verse,

> "You've been carried away and your turn has come
> When you lose by your own fault, who can help you?"[55]

The rest of Hafiz's life has been detailed by the illustrious Prince Sultan Husayn[56] in his book *Meetings of the Lovers* (*Majalis al-'ushaq*). There is no room to go into it here. Following this exchange I gave my tongue in praise to the Emperor and said,

> "O God, as long as the Sun and Moon shall be
> May Jahangir son of Akbar remain King."

---

[55]The legend of Hafiz's meeting with Timur is well-known, but probably apocryphal. Mutribi's association of the story with his own experience with Jahangir is certainly an intentional reflection of the Mughal emperor's attachment to the Timurid legacy.

[56]Sultan Husayn Bayqara, Timurid ruler of Herat from 1470-1506.

Second Meeting: Jahangir Asks For News From Samarqand

An evening happier than the rising star of fortune
Scattered fragrant musk over the Beloved's oppressive face

I had the honor of waiting upon the Emperor; he beckoned me to draw close. Present were the Prince of the World Sultan Shahryar[57] and such nobles of the Steadfast State as Navvab Asaf Khan[58], Khwaja Abu'l Hasan-i Divan[59], Iradat Khan[60], Khavvas Khan[61], Bahadur Khan of Transoxiana[62] and others. His Majesty showed me the kindness of asking a few questions. First he asked about the condition of the mausoleum of his majesty Timur, where the tomb of the Emperor's great honored forefathers is and which in Samarqand is known as the Gur-i Amir. I replied,

"I have told everything of the condition of that mausoleum in my book, *The Beautiful Book of Jahangir*, the very title and completion date of which is an expression of this very thing. I

---

[57]Shah Jahan's third son, Jahangir's grandson.

[58]Nur Jahan's brother. See Anil Kumar, *Asaf Khan and His Times*, Patna, 1986; also *Ma'asir al-'umara'*, i, 287-295.

[59]*Tuzuk*, i, 79, 80, 103, 172, 192, 202, 219, 221, 256, 260, 282, 287, 318, 320; ii, 5, 82, 127, 155, 163, 193, 220, 251, 254; *Ma'asir al-'umara'*, i, 128-130.

[60]*Ma'asir al-'umara'*, i, 315-319.

[61]*Ma'asir al-'umara'*, i, 467-471.

[62]Apparently Abu'l Biy Uzbek (see Chapter Eighteen) is meant here. See *Akbar-Nama*, iii, 820, 839 (where he appears as Abu'l Baqa); *Tuzuk*, i, 234-5; *Ma'asir al-'umara'*, i, 400.

hope that this will become known to His Excellency the Divine Viceregent."[63]

The Emperor then asked the color of Timur's sepulchre, and whether it was indeed made of a slab of black stone. He showed me a stone and asked,

"Is that blessed stone as black as this? Because I've never even seen a torch beam as bright as this, if I'm not mistaken."

"That blessed stone is brighter than this, and shinier," I replied. "It's so shiny you can see your face in it.

"Apparently," I went on, "it's not a slab of stone after all. My son Muhammad 'Ali told me that when they showed it to him, someone said it wasn't a stone, but rather black gold. I said to my son, 'O, son! All my life I've denied the existence of such black gold, but now it's become clear that it does in fact exist.'[64] The reason for my denial was that in the shrine of the Most Enlightened Prince Qusam ibn Abbas[65] an eight-part stone was erected over the entry arch bearing the following inscription:

'O you, who in this place find your heart's desire
Recite the Fatiha for the craftsman 'Ali of Tabriz.'

"During the reign of Baqi Muhammad Khan[66], Javanmard 'Ali Khan had a son of Sultan Sa'id Khan's household assis-

---

[63]It would appear that Jahangir has not had the time to read Mutribi's long-labored gift.

[64]Actually Timur's sepulchre is of black jade.

[65]A cousin of the Prophet Muhammad, who apparently came to Samarqand with an Arab army in 676. He died in Central Asia, but according to legend he was not killed and became immortal, hence the name of his shrine *Shah-i Zinda* ("The Living King") in Samarqand to which Mutribi is referring. See V.V. Barthold, *Turkestan Down to the Mongol Invasion*, London: Luzac, 1977, 91-2.

[66]Ashtarkhanid ruler of Transoxiana and Balkh from 1601-1604. But this would seem to be an anachronism, as Javanmard 'Ali died in 1578, during the reign of 'Abdullah Khan.

tant[67] Shams al-Din Muhammad thrown from the top of the
Ulugh Beg seminary[68] as a punishment. As they were carrying
him up to the roof he recited the following quatrain:

> 'Help! Time is up for my poor self
> The hunter has got me in a noose
> For the sigh of what poor self
> Have I unjustly destroyed a hundred homes?'

"The reason for this event is that the son, whose name was
Mirak, had read the quatrain on the aforementioned stone, and
the meaning he gleaned was that from this stone one could ob-
tain one's wishes. One night he brought a ladder and removed
the stone from its place and carried it off. When the custodians
of the shrine realized what had happened they informed Baqi
Khan of it. Mirak was sought out and found, and when the stone
was studied it was found to be made of shiny black gold.

"Your humble servant was in Bukhara when this incident
became known and now, in the year 1036, the original place of
that stone at the top of the archway is empty, as anyone who
looks will notice."

Following this discussion, the royal command was issued
that I be given a robe of honor.[69] A top-quality turban and
Kashmiri shawl were given to me, and a gold-embroidered robe,
a sash with good golden thread and decorated skirt to my son
Muhammad 'Ali. After we had been thus honored, the Emperor
said,

"We also said we would give you a horse and saddle; we
will do that tomorrow."

After all this kindness, I offered the following verse, which
contains the date of the event:

---

[67]*Kirak-yirak*; I am grateful to Devin DeWeese for suggesting an
interpretation for this obscure Turkic term, which would seem to refer
to a person responsible for procuring household supplies.

[68]One of the three seminaries of the Registan square in Samarqand.

[69]Mutribi is satisfying Jahangir's keen interest in his own ancestral
connections in Central Asia.

"In the court of the King of Religion, Jahangir
Praise be to Allah that I was given an audience
Gold and turban and horse and saddle
Were granted me by royal favor
In recognition of these kindnesses
My mind composed the chronogram, 'Divine Honor'".[70]

Having received permission to return another day, I said,

"O God, as long as the Sun and Moon shall be
May Jahangir son of Akbar remain King."

---

[70]The numerical value of the phrase *tashrif-i ilahi* is 1036. There is a
pun on the "robe of honor" given to visitors by the Emperor.

Third Meeting: Some Marvels

Another night the King of the Seven Lands
Sat upon the great golden throne

I came to kiss the royal threshold. The grandees of the State and His Highness' nobles were all assembled. Frankish merchants had laid tribute before His Majesty's luminous gaze. In the hand of the Divine Viceregent there was a small book a little bigger than four fingers, comprising twelve yellowed folios. It was locked and a key was set upon it. The Emperor called me forward and asked, "What book might this be?"

Since I didn't for the life of me know, I replied, "O Qibla of the World, I know not what book it is."

He unlocked it with his own hand and showed it to me, and said, "Whatever is written with this pen on these pages appears black; when you rub it the page becomes white again. If you write again and rub it again, it will be in the same condition.[71] If all the books in the world were written in this manner, then they could all be erased!"

I was amazed and stupefied by this discussion. Then to educate me, he took the pen and wrote out a couplet (representative of his sound nature) on the page:

"We wrote a message upon a rose petal
Perhaps the Zephyr will bring it to him".

---

[71]Apparently pencils were a novelty at Jahangir's court, brought by European visitors.

Then that Truth-Worshipping hand erased it and showed it to me; the page was as white as it had been at first. Next he jokingly asked me,

"If I were to sell you this book for one rupee, would you accept?"

I replied, "O Qibla of the World, this must be some kind of talisman made in the form of a book, and it would bring some harm upon me."

He said, "It's no talisman, and it won't bring any harm to anybody."

"I don't have a rupee on me," I said.

He chuckled and gave it to me. Now out of humble respect I keep that book with me. If it brings me luck on my way home to Turan when I get permission to leave the court of the Divine Viceregent, I will give it to Imam Quli Bahadur Khan[72] as a present.

In the time of our former ruler 'Abdullah Khan, Mawlana Jalali Tabib who was a skillful physician and had complete knowledge of magic and talismans, had constructed a trunk in the Ghazian quarter of Bukhara which was never empty of rarities. I once went to see that trunk; everyone used to come and be amused by it. The trunk's height was that of a tall man. He had installed that trunk in the center of his house so that one could go around the trunk and examine its exterior. There wasn't a hole visible anywhere, except that on the top of the trunk there was a secret hatch and a lion's head sticking out from inside the trunk. There was a bronze bowl attached to an iron rod, and facing the lion's head was a wooden horse. Below the hatch there was an iron rod with an ape sitting astride it which told the time of day. In the left hand of the ape was a small bronze bowl, and an iron rod was attached to his right hand. When an hour of day or night had passed, the rod would push the right hand of the monkey and make him drink from the goblet, and a bell would sound to indicate that an hour had passed.

Mawlana Jalali also had a ball made of seven metals which he would hand to one of his visitors. That person would throw

---

[72] r. 1612-1642.

the ball into the mouth of the horse; the ball would go through the horse's mouth into the trunk and fall to the bottom, and make a loud noise audible to everybody present. Then the ball of seven metals would rise up from the bottom of the trunk to the top, making a whirring noise. When it got to the top it would come out of the lion's mouth and fall into the goblet; the hatch in the middle would open up and inside the trunk a throne would appear, a man sitting on it with his two arms stretched out. About his two hands would be wound a sheet of paper. The magician would take down the paper, and all the Master's thoughts would be written on it, for example advice on going into business, or whether to go or not to go on a journey, or whether what you were lacking would come or not come, or if the sick would get healthy or not, or if one should undertake such-and-such a task or not, and so on. When the magician finished reading the paper, the hatch would close up and the trunk would look just as it had before.

Mawlana Jalali was a very good poet, and these two couplets are representative:

> I left your neighborhood; my heart is still branded with misery
> A hundred thoughts of your curly hair still fill my head
> My heart is like a tulip cleft by the sword of your injustice
> My eyes are still bloodshot from my bleeding heart.

Fourth Meeting: Maktub Khan

Another day that the face of the King brightened the world[73]
The slave army fled the battlefield

I came before the throne of the peerless world-turning King. He said, "I very much liked your book."
    In gratitude for this good fortune I recited this couplet:

> "O God, as long as the Sun and Moon shall be
> May Jahangir son of Akbar remain King."

I had composed this couplet in the style of Yadgar Qurchi:

> "How penitently I take my lip from the cup
> Yet I prostrate myself before the face of my idol beneath the wood of the vine."

The Emperor said, "Where is Maktub Khan?"
Maktub Khan was present.
"Maktub Khan!" he said. "You know how Yadgar Qurchi's poem goes:
> 'Since my lips have repented from the cup
> Yet, I'll fashion my old man's walking stick from the wood of the vine...'[74]

---

[73]This would appear to be a reference to Jahangir's *laqab*, Nur al-Din ("Light of the Faith").

[74]Jahangir is vaunting his Central Asian roots through his knowledge of Central Asian poets.

Maktub Khan stared uncomfortably, then tried to begin. When I realized his state, I said, "Your health, King! Maktub Khan doesn't know Yadgar Qurchi.[75] But Yadgar Qurchi knows Maktub Khan, because Maktub Khan is the forerunner and Yadgar Qurchi came after him."

The Divine Viceregent seemed pleased, and showed me the favor of asking me the correct version. I recited:

"When I take my lips from the cup in repentance
The wine drunk, I fashion excuses from the wood of the vine."

Maktub Khan is one of the most privileged of the trustworthy servants of the Court, and for a long time had offered his life in service to the Emperor and continued to serve him honorably. He is currently in charge of the royal library as well as the painters' atelier. What fortune for him could be greater than this, that in the Divine Viceregent's royal memoirs, the *Book of Jahangir*— which is the ultimate expression of that peerless enlightened king's nature— he is described positively.[76] When Jahangir acceded to the throne he ordered that the poets should commemorate the event with chronograms. When Maktub Khan composed a good one, the Emperor liked it and put it into the royal memoirs. It went thus:

King of kings Jahangir, a second Timur
Sat in justice on the victorious throne
Success, fortune, victory, pomp, and triumph
Are wrapped around him to serve with joy
This is the date of his accession,
When fortune puts its head at the feet of the second Timur.[77]

Even though the honorable Khan is nearly eighty years of age, the meadow of his speech still blossoms with insight from the rain of the clouds of meaning, and the richness of expression

---

[75]That is, his poetry.

[76]*Tuzuk-i Jahangiri*, i, 12.

[77] The last line forms the chronogram.

in his pearly offerings is striking. He was especially skilled at rhyming couplets. In the following quatrain he nicely expresses the weakness of his own old age:

> From weakness I fall from the shirt's thread
> And from head to toe, the wind of speech blows me down
> Once my shadow fell from me to earth
> Now from my shadow I fall to earth.

Since his family origins were the pure soil of Shiraz, he used the pen-name, "Farsi".[78] He is very good-natured, eloquent, polite, and humble. Among all the swarms of poets in India I haven't seen anyone as companionable, pure-hearted, and warm as he is. The following verses are representative of his poetic skill:

> Since your cruciform curls became the guide of hearts
> Their voice has soothed my heart and soul
> Our turning is not like Heaven's
> Heaven's returns to itself, and mine to the door of the heart

> Know from the start how charming and beautiful you are, O boy
> Don't on any account give away that telltale wink
> A thousand blood-red tulips emerge from the heart of the soil
> If from my eye one drops to the ground

> I had news of the blooming flower at the stroke of dawn
> It had no news from him, yet I had news from it
> There was further proof in the beauty of your handwriting[79]
> You wrote a page from memory; I learned the lesson
> I read a few verses from the Quran of your beauty
> Once I'm holding you, I forget all I've learned

> My heart is cut through by an eyelash
> This is not a skill that can be learned
> Don't waste a teardrop

---

[78]Shiraz is the capital of Fars province.

[79]A pun with "peach-fuzz" (*khat*), a stock trait of adolescent boys.

For these priceless jewels must be conserved
The tumult of love is the very essence of heat
Every breath is like a flame
I asked him, "who's the one who loves you?"
He said, "Farsi, burning himself alive"

Tulips sprout from thorns and roses from mud
If the meadow sees your rose face
I'll use my pupil as mascara; perhaps
He'll forget and notice me.

Fifth Meeting: Truth is a Virtue

An evening brighter than the morning of youth
A harvest of happiness and good times

The Divine Viceregent's swarm of attendants were all gathered in their assigned places. His Majesty asked me, "Do you know Mirza Baqi Anjomani?"

I replied, "He was the son of one of 'Abdullah Khan's prefects; he came to India to enter the service of Emperor Akbar. He earned distinction for composing a quatrain on the occasion of Emperor Akbar's falling off a horse. The quatrain goes like this:

'Your noble steed steps through the heavens;
Don't fault him for missing two steps
He felt weak beneath the stirrups of your glory
He hit his knees and fell helpless to the ground'".

His Majesty asked, "How did you hear what became of him once he came to India?"

I replied, "In Samarqand I heard that after Emperor Akbar passed away, he decided to make the pilgrimage, but I don't know if he ever made it to Mecca or not. Recently since I've been blessed with the opportunity to spend time in Lahore one of the poets, who goes by the pen-name of 'the Brahmin', told me that on a pilgrimage caravan he shared the same saddle with Mirza Baqi Anjomani, and that he made the pilgrimage but then died somewhere."

The Emperor vehemently denied this, and said, "'the Brahmin' lied. Mirza Baqi didn't make the pilgrimage; he lived and died in my service."

Since "the Brahmin" lied to me I did not include any of his
verses in this book. From this I discovered that the Divine
Viceregent, in accordance with the hadith "The liar is not from
my community"[80], gives no mind to liars, and that nothing but
forthrightness holds any weight with him. And in this sense he
makes sure people get what they deserve.

> Be truthful that you might be saved
> Truth from you is victory from the Creator
> Sugarcane is nourished by His truth
> The rose grows crooked from the thorn in its breast.

> Dishonesty will make you lose everything
> You'll be saved from every sorrow if you're honest.

> Because the letter "A" (*alif*) is straight, it is the center of *jan*
> (soul)
> Because the letter "U" (*vav*) is crooked, it is the center of *khun*
> (blood).

They say a sufi was on his way to Mecca, carrying five hundred dirhams and a single piece of bread. A group of highwaymen intercepted him and said, "Hey, sufi, whatever you've got
under your arm bring it out." The sufi said, I've got five hundred
dirhams and one piece of bread," and brought them out. "Don't
lie," said the highwaymen. "Don't you have anything else?"
They searched him, but didn't find anything other than what
he'd said. Since in his speech they detected the aroma of truth,
they took pity on him, put the dirhams and the bread back under
his arm, and left. Indeed, nothing brings better fruit than truth-
fulness. Well it is said that ignorant people who diverge from
the path of truth will incline towards deceitfulness.

Accordingly it appears that the Divine Viceregent wished to
test me. He asked me, "Do you know Abu'l Biy Uzbek?"

---

[80]Ar. *Al-kadhdhab la ummati.* The phrase can also be read, "*Al-
kadhdhab la amti,*" or "The liar is not on the straight path," which also
goes with the story which follows. In hadith literature "the Liar" is
often equated with the Antichrist (*al-Dajjal*).

"Which Abu'l Biy?" I replied. "The one who was governor of Samarqand for a few days during the reign of Baqi Muhammad Khan, then became governor of Qandahar? If you mean that Abu'l Biy, then I know him."

He said, "That's the one I mean." Then he had two men brought before me, one white-bearded and the other rather dark.

"Indeed, that white-bearded fellow doesn't look like Abu'l Biy, unless he's aged a lot. But that dark one doesn't look like him either."

He smiled and said, "Actually, neither one is Abu'l Biy. One is Afzal Khan and the other is Musavi Khan."

Another time, however, when the Divine Viceregent was showing portraits of the Uzbek khans, I recognized Abu'l Biy among them. Since Abu'l Biy himself was present, he exclaimed, "The mulla doesn't know me!" I replied, "I know you well, but you don't know me." The Divine Viceregent said, "We trust in the discernment of the mulla."

I replied,

"O God, as long as the Sun and Moon shall be
May Jahangir son of Akbar remain King."

Sixth Meeting: Jahangir's Lunar Weighing Ceremony

Another day brought by the sun of the World-Illuminator
Fortune placed its forehead in prostration upon the dust of the
path of the King

It was the celebration of His Majesty's lunar birthday. The crowds got dressed up in their finest and thronged to see. How can one explain the finery and exquisiteness of this celebration, when the mind is stupefied by the sight of that auspicious occasion? That day after the weighing ceremony and the distribution of gold and jewels and *bakhsheesh*, the Emperor honored your humble servant with a gift of two trayloads of *tangas*, an almond of silver, and folios of miniature paintings; all in all nearly two thousand things, which he poured into my bag with his own Justice-Worshipping hand.[81]

O God, as long as the Sun and Moon shall be
May Jahangir son of Akbar remain King!

Then he asked, "Have you prepared anything in honor of our celebration?"
I recited the following quatrain:

"The celebration of the King of kings of intellect became confused

---

[81] It was a Mughal custom to distribute the Emperor's weight in gold and jewels to the population on the occasion of his lunar and solar birthdays. An English ambassador, Sir Thomas Roe, describes Jahangir's lunar weighing ceremony in his 1617 account (Sir Thomas Roe, *The Embassy of Sir Thomas Roe to the Court of the Great Mogul 1615-1619*, ed. William Foster, London, 1899, 411-412).

And from its confusion the spheres turned upside down
When the Emperor sat in the scales, I said,
'The Sun of the World is in the house of Libra!'"[82]

The Emperor applauded and gave me another hundred rupees, and said, "I'll give you the horse and the spending money I
promised now. What kind of horse do you want, an 'Iraqi or a
Turani one? Do you want a velvet saddle or one of broadcloth?"

"O Qibla of the World," I replied, "I'd like whichever horse
is more expensive."

"'Iraqi horses are more expensive," he said, "but they're
very spirited and fast- you might not be able to stay on him![83]
What kind of saddle do you want, velvet or broadcloth?"

"O Qibla of the World," I replied, "Whichever is more expensive!"

"You tell me which is more expensive," he said.

"O Qibla of the World," I replied, I should think the velvet
one is more expensive."

"That's right," he said. "But a velvet saddle gets wet in the
rain, whereas while a broadcloth saddle is less expensive, it's
waterproof."

"O Qibla of the World," I replied, "the monsoon season is
still far off."

So he had a dark, docile horse and velvet saddle brought as
gifts for me.

> World-possessor, world-benefactor, Jahangir is that Holy
> Warrior (*ghazi*)
> King of kings who gave favor and beauty to the four corners
> of the world
>
> Beneath the nine-pillared heavens in this six-door house
> Like him, born of the mother, the four elements
> was no one born but lesser in generosity
> Out of kindness he gave this humble servant a horse
> Whose speed even the wind couldn't match

---

[82]Libra=*mizan*=scales.

[83]Mutribi is seventy years old, after all!

Since he made me happy with generosity and a turban and gold and clothes

O God, grant him countless years of life in the world.[84]

---

[84]Lit., "may the years of his life in the world be counted with generosity" (*ilahi sal-i 'umrash dar jahan mahsub-i ihsan bad*). The numerical value of *mahsub* is 120; in other words, may he live to be 120.

Seventh Meeting: The World's Biggest Sugar Block

Another day lit by the Sun of the World
The world lit up by royal splendor

I had the pleasure of kissing the threshold of the Divine Vicere-gent. I saw before His Enlightened Majesty a huge block of sugar— in all my life, I'd never seen a sugar block so big. I would guess that according to Bukhara weights it was half a maund.[85] It was set upon a silver stool. The Emperor called me to his side and asked,

"Have you ever seen a block of sugar like this in Tran-soxiana?"

"Not in my lifetime," I answered.

"We haven't seen such a one in India either," he said. "Today our faithful servant Muhammad Husayn Khalaf brought it from Lucknow, which is one month's journey from the joyous realm of Lahore. He brought it before the foot of our heavenly throne, and we are giving it to you." I thanked him appropri-ately.

He asked me, "Are you going to use this block of sugar here in Lahore, or will you take it home with you?"

"O Qibla of the World," I replied, "if I eat it all in Lahore I'll get sick. It would be better if I take it back to Samarqand."

The Emperor asked, "Is there anyone in Transoxiana who would deserve such a block of sugar?"

I replied, "Two people would be. One is the ruler of Turan, Imam Quli Khan; the other is His Honorable Excellency."

---

[85]A maund is equal to 2.334 kilograms (Thackston, *Babur-nama*, 350, note 98).

"I don't know who this His Honorable Excellency is," said the Emperor.

"The blessed name of His Honorable Excellency is Master Hashim Muhammad Dihbidi[86], a short account of whom appears in the *Jahangir-nama* so wonderfully expressed by the fragrant pen of the Divine Viceregent and Shadow of the Almighty," I explained.

He replied, "I myself am one of his devotees and his sincere servant,[87] especially these days since I threw 'Mardud Khan' out of my court and gave him the title 'Mardud Khan'[88]. The reason for his being thrown out is that some of Khwaja Hashim's followers had brought me some hunting falcons,[89] and

---

[86]He was hereditary leader of the Dihbidi family of sufi masters of Samarqand; see my, "The Naqshbandi Connections of the Mughal Emperors", *Journal of Islamic Studies* 7/2 (1996), 233.

[87]It was common for rulers, especially in Central Asia where the Naqshbandi sufi order played an active political role, to maintain a fiction of discipleship and submission to the instruction of a spiritual guide. Jahangir is clearly placing himself within this tradition.

[88]Lit., "the Khan who was thrown out".

[89]Central Asia was known for these birds, which were frequently sent to India as presents for the elite. See, for example, *Tuzuk*, ii, 10; Inayat Khan, *Shah Jahan-nama*, tr. A.R. Fuller, ed. W.E. Begley and Z.A. Desai, Delhi: Oxford University Press, 1990; 148, 244, 536.

that fool didn't bring it to our enlightened attention. When he learned we had found out about it, he came to us in order to say insulting things about Khwaja Hashim's emissaries. What's more, he said the falcons weren't all that good. For this reason, he did not remain in the ranks of my servants; before long his inner soul died, and was completely extinguished. On the other hand, our respect for Khwaja Hashim's emissaries was only increased. God willing, we'll make it up to them. When you pay your respects to the Master, convey our apologies to him."

I replied,

> "O God, as long as the Sun and Moon shall be
> May Jahangir son of Akbar remain King."

Eighth Meeting: The *Surkhab*

Another day that in this realm of pleasure
Golden idols appear from the Fountain of Light

I came to kiss the threshold of the Divine Viceregent. Since it
was the time for discussion amongst His Excellency's grandees
and nobles, having offered my respects I sat to the side of the
assembly. After a time His Majesty showed the kindness of
calling me forward. In front of him was a bird called a *surk-hab*[90] that had been hunted. His Majesty looked at me and said,
"Yesterday we were out hunting. This *surkhab* flew up, and
I took my rifle and said, 'This is for Preacher Mutribi!' We fired
and hit it. We've been keeping it for you; it's yours."
I bowed and said,

"O God, as long as the Sun and Moon shall be
May Jahangir son of Akbar remain King."

When I took the *surkhab* on my arm, His Majesty said, "We
have done something for you; what have you done for us?" I
offered him this quatrain:

"The King, whose face shone upon the sun and moon
The cloud of his magnanimity watered the field of the heart

---

[90]The ruddy sheldrake or Brahminy duck (Salim Ali, *The Book of
Indian Birds*, 10th ed., Bombay: Bombay Natural History Society,
1977).

When he saw that I'm a sufi, he put not *surkh ab*[91] on my elderly head
But, rather, a *surkhab*."

A hundred rupees were given in reward.

---

[91]"Red water," or color into his pale face. Alternatively, it may be a reference to menstrual blood.

Ninth Meeting: Of Tasty Duck and New Year's Revelry

Another day, that the world received the sun's rays
The shield was taken from its revolutions, and the sword from
the sun

I came to kiss the threshold of the Glory of the Spheres the Divine Viceregent and stood in attendance. Two ducks, caught from the hunt, had been brought before His Noble Highness. He turned his attention to this insignificant person and called me forward, and pointed to one of the ducks. My understanding was that he intended to give me both ducks. When I tried to take them, he laughed and held up one finger, meaning I should take one and leave the other. I put one of them back.

When I got home I had the duck stuffed and cooked. I'll tell you, that duck's meat was so delicious and tender that it made me think of the Quranic verse, "And the flesh of birds is what they desire."[92] You might say that Indian ducks are tastier than those of Transoxiana— or perhaps it was just that this duck was shot by His Majesty.

My esteemed father once told me of a man named Mulla Sham'-i Yak Puli who traveled to India in the time of the Honored Emperor Humayun[93]; he spent some time there and then returned to Transoxiana and became a boon companion of 'Abd al-Latif Khan[94] son of Kuchkunji Khan. He used to say that Indian ducks were the tastiest there were. For that reason in

---

[92]Qur'an, 56:21.
[93]Jahangir's grandfather; r. 1530-55.
[94]r. 1540-52.

Samarqand he had duck meat at every opportunity and never spent an hour of his life without wine.

> The cup of wine is my oldest companion
> We talk and sit together; the ritual is this
> If one day I don't drink wine, I'll die
> You might say that bitter wine is the sweetness of my life

The days of the New Year[95] are a time of special celebration and festivity for the people of Samarqand. And what days they are! Young partiers get dressed up in costumes and drink wine and have fun, as the Honored Emperor Humayun described in the following couplet:

> Make whatever you can of New Year's night
> Since by day sorrow is your daily bread.

And similarly, His Majesty Emperor Zahir al-din Babur said:

> New year and new spring and wine and happy sweethearts
> Babur, enjoy yourself, for this world won't come again.[96]

Emperor Akbar, likewise, put it well:

> On New Year's eve I got silly and dead drunk
> Day and night were the same to cup-worshipping me.

Actually, it was for the sake of wine-drinking that one day an infraction occurred. 'Abd al-Latif Khan decreed that during the New Year's celebrations no one should take wine out of Samarqand to drink it, and that to do so would be considered a crime. During the celebrations the Khan's guards were keeping such careful watch at the gates of the city that there was no way anyone could take wine out.

---

[95]*No ruz*, an ancient Iranian festival held at the vernal equinox.

[96]This couplet was actually composed by the Emperor's namesake and cousin, Babur Qalandar son of Prince Baysunghur (*Rawzat al-salatin*, 93).

But Mulla Sham' along with the seminary students and cer-
tain villains of the town devised a scheme wherein he sent the
young partiers out ahead, telling them to wait outside of town
and he'd bring the wine out to them by some ruse. Then he put a
tub of wine into a coffin, tore his shirt, wrapped his head in
black and put his turban onto the coffin. He got another group of
villains to carry the coffin; tearing his shirt he ran back and forth
beside the coffin, lamenting and crying out, "O my brother Akhund Mulla Tubby![97] Ah, my dear Mulla Tubby! My faithful
Mulla Tubby! Why did you have to die! Alas that you must be
buried on such a day! Who can I tell of your misery? If only I
could go to 'Abd al-Latif Khan and complain about the Angel of
Death!"

He cried and wailed like you wouldn't believe. In this way
he got the wine past the guards and out the city gates, and
brought it to his friends. They passed around the cup, and as the
drinking session heated up, they all started wailing songs of la-
ment.

By chance 'Abd al-Latif Khan, who was out celebrating
with the nobles and grandees by firing a cannon, heard this
drunken singing. "What's all that ruckus?" he asked. "Mulla
Sham'-i Yak Puli is out drinking with his friends," he was told.
The order was given to have them rounded up. When the group
of friends were brought to him, the Khan said, "Tell me honestly
how you got the wine out of the city without the guards notic-
ing." They explained it to him. The Khan liked their story so
much he pardoned them and gave them presents.

The point of this story was to illustrate how tasty Indian
ducks are.

O God, as long as the Sun and Moon shall be

---

[97]The pun is clearer in Persian: "*khik*" means a wineskin, and "*khiki*"
means chubby.

May Jahangir son of Akbar remain King.

Tenth Meeting: The Best Color
for a Slave Boy

A night, like the dawn's rays striking
The world brighter than the rays of the sun

I came before the threshold of the Refuge of the Angels. After I had performed the appropriate greetings, the Divine Viceregent spoke very kindly to me: "Preacher! What kind of slave-boy is best, white-skinned or dark?"

I replied, "Different people have different tastes. Some like black, others prefer white. But as the wise have said,

'The Lover will find out everything about the Beloved
Whether the face be pleasing, or the form ugly.'"

His Majesty said, "I meant your personal preference— what have others got to do with us?"

I replied, "O Qibla of the World, let me see and I'll tell you."

"Look to your right and to your left," he said. "Maybe then you'll see!"

No sooner had he spoken than by my right was standing a black-skinned youth, and what a soul-destroyer! I lost my heart at the sight of him.

A Hindu youth stole my wretched heart
He stole away my resolve and my peace
Wisdom, knowledge, patience and forebearance
He stole away all with his sweet laughter

To my right stood a white-skinned boy; he too was so good and delicate that I couldn't believe my eyes.

> O white-skinned Moon! On such a good night
> So amazingly agreeable by the light of the candle
> You're stealing helpless Mutribi's heart
> With your winks and loveable coquettishness

> Don't tell me to look at the meadow's floral display
> My heart is your captive; what have I to do with anything else?

I kept looking back and forth from my right side to my left until I couldn't stand it anymore. "O Qibla of the World!" I said, "First I was captivated by the black, then by the white. These colors have gotten mixed up and made another color; I can no longer tell if the white youth is white or the black one black... indeed it must be a kind of candy-green color that gives the best taste."

"Then we'll have to say it's this tasty green color!" he said, and recited the following quatrain:

> "O you who are so tasty
> You've sifted the atoms of life through with taste
> You've made tasty the juices of the heart
> With such an arousing appearance as yours."

I said, "That reminds me of the saying of the Greats that His Excellency the Refuge of Prophecy (peace and blessings be upon him) once said, 'Even if my brother Joseph (peace be upon him) was the pinnacle of beauty, I too have charm!'"[98]

"That's just what I meant," the Emperor replied.

> O God, as long as the Sun and Moon shall be
> May Jahangir son of Akbar remain King.

---

[98]The biblical figure of Joseph (Yusuf), whose story constitutes chapter 12 of the Qur'an, is treated in Muslim legend as the paradigm of beauty.

At the time the following quatrain occurred to me, although
I didn't share it with the Divine Viceregent:

In the land of India I saw a ray of light
The beam of which fell upon my chest
Was this lovely face for real
Or a trick of India I saw in my sleep?

Eleventh Meeting: By the Light of the Moon

> An evening as long as the hair of beauties
> It seemed to be a work of the imagination

One evening the World-Decorating Moon raised his head from his collar and brought it to court; the world was illuminated by his light.

> When the moon became a bowl of cheese
> Our street became like channels of milk

The Peerless King had gone out to look at the moonlight, in a place where all the walls were white, and cloth merchants had laid out white silks on the ground; the World-Protecting Emperor himself was dressed in a white robe of honor. The grandees of the State and His Majesty's nobles were standing at his service, also dressed in white, and a throne of white marble had been set up for this ceremony. His Majesty sat on that Throne of Fortune of the Garb of Reliance. Your humble servant having been uninformed of the occasion, not knowing only white was to be worn, I presented myself at the threshold of Holy Refuge. Several officials blocked my way and said, "The command of the Noble One whom the World Obeys is that one must come to the Lofty Session dressed in white. One who has not dressed in a white robe may not pass."

Since time was tight I couldn't get hold of a white robe. Therefore I told the following quatrain to that sweet-voiced nightingale Fasih Khan, so that during the Lofty Session he might present it to the Divine Viceregent:

> "Tonight when the smoke of wisdom rises from dreams

The horizons have found light from the moon
By the light of the moon, the King appeared
Or was it the sun, coming to look at the moonlight?"

Once the quatrain had made my situation known, the royal order was given for me to be dressed in a fine white turban and beautiful white robe and brought into the presence of the Divine Viceregent. As soon as I had been honored with the robe and joined the ranks of humble servitude, I bowed and said,

"O God, as long the Sun and Moon shall be
May Jahangir son of Akbar remain King."

Twelfth Meeting: Camel and Oryx Fights

Another night full of fireworks
Pleasant companionship on all sides

I came in submission before the Divine Viceregent. All around I saw the royal family lit up by a thousand five hundred lanterns; the torches were without end. The Divine Viceregent was enjoying himself watching camel and oryx fights. The royal Obeyed-by-the-World command was issued for a mad camel to be brought out, and fighting oryxes were brought out as well. First came the oryx fights; one might say they brought to the mind of your poor servant the meaning of the Master's couplet,

"Your eyebrows and your eyes, O Chinese face
Are deer clashing antlers out of wrath."

Next we proceeded to watch the camel fights. Never in Transoxiana did I see such a thing. Since I'd never seen such a wonderful fight before, I am unable to recount all of its qualities. Even so I can say that the sight of it thrilled the heart, and this was no illusion. Therefore I composed this quatrain for His Majesty:

Anyone made unhappy by this world
Even though his heart be blacker than tar
The camel fight of Emperor Jahangir
Would brighten the mirror of his dark heart

Then he asked me, "Have you ever seen such camel and oryx fights in Transoxiana?"
"I've seen camel fights," I replied, "but not oryx fights."

"This type of oryx doesn't exist in Transoxiana," he said, "so how could you have seen them fight?" Then he said, "I arranged these fights for your benefit."

I replied,

"O God, as long as the Sun and Moon shall be
May Jahangir son of Akbar remain King."

Thirteenth Meeting: The Eye of the Lover

The night amber-scented like the hair of beauties
Its scent perfumed the nose of the heart and soul

I was in attendance with the attendants of the Divine Viceregent.
He was reclining upon the Throne of Good Fortune, preparing
for bed in a way which made me think of the noble verse, "And
We have made your sleep a repose"[99]. During this time he made
up a couplet and wrote it down on a piece of paper and gave it to
your humble servant, and said, "Make up a response in the same
rhyme and meter."[100]
His couplet went,

> "The eye of the Lover is like a lantern
> It won't sleep till it's dead".

As God is my witness, without missing a beat I replied,

> "The heart of the Lover is like a kebab
> It won't dry out till it's burned".

Some unbelieving nobody, obviously seeking his own profit,
said, "That couplet is by the Master!" Hearing this, I recited another couplet:

---

[99]Qur'an 78:9.

[100]This practice of composing extemporaneous responses in verse,
called *mujavaba* or *istiqbal*, was common both during improvisation
sessions at court and in correspondence.

"The eye of the Lover is like the sea
The depth of which people cannot gauge".

Despite the unbeliever's remark, the Divine Viceregent said, "*That* couplet isn't by the Master." I recited another couplet:

"Whoever is in love with the Beloved
I'll tell you straight: he'll never get to sleep".

That convinced the nobody, and he shut up. When the Divine Viceregent had fallen asleep, the following couplet came to my mind:

"Wherever there is a broken heart
Kings will soothe them with kindness".

When he awoke from untroubled sleep I presented myself. In his kindness he told me, "You have your wits together. I'm going to show you a lot of favor. I'm going to take you along with me to the wonderful land of Kashmir. On the way to Kashmir, abundant favors are going to come to you. We're just waiting for the arrival of 'Abd al-Rahim Khwaja Juybari."[101] I bowed and said,

"O God, as long as the Sun and Moon shall be
May Jahangir son of Akbar remain king."

Immediately a gift of the sum of two hundred rupees was given. Then he said,
"I was reciting this couplet as I was dropping off to sleep; if the excellent courtiers would recite while I'm awake it would be nice. You seem to know everything about poetry; I don't know exactly who it was that came up with this nice couplet:

'The eye of the Lover is like a cloud

---

[101]A Naqshbandi sufi shaykh of the Juybari family of Bukhara. Imam Quli Khan had sent him to propose an alliance against the Safavids.

It won't sleep till it's cried.'"

The Most Erudite Doctor Masih al-Zaman[102] expressed just this sentiment:

"The eye of the Lover is like a spring
Its water won't let it go to sleep."

And Mawlana Darvish Mansur Samarqandi likewise said:

"The eye of the Lover is like mercury
Only once it's stilled does it get to sleep."

My esteemed mother once told me, "Your maternal grandfather used to recite poetry in his sleep, blind as he was. They say that blind people don't have two eyes and a nose on their faces, and that their faces are featureless. Rather, they have slits for a mouth and a hole for a nose. It's as Almighty God revealed in the Holy Qur'an in this regard (the speech of the Almighty): 'I heal him who was born blind, and the leper, and I raise the dead'[103].

"He had the nickname 'the Seer'. Anything that seeing people could do, he could do. Your grandfather knew the art of tailoring— which was the occupation of His Excellency Idris[104] (peace be upon him). He could thread the needle and sew clothing, and go out out to buy whatever he needed for tailoring and come back again, and along the way he would browse and visit just like seeing people do.

"Poetry used to come to him. Your grandfather told me, 'When I recite poetry in my sleep, write it down so I can remember it when I'm awake.'"

This couplet of his became well-known:

---

[102]A.k.a. Hakim Sadra; *Tuzuk*, i, 155, 267, 374; ii, 217; *Ma'asir al-'umara'*, ii, 662-664.

[103]Qur'an 3: 49.

[104]According to legend Idris was the inventor of the art of sewing, and was looked upon as the patron saint of tailors.

My aching heart is nourished by a sea of blood
We devotees see for the sake of God, as we've been brought
up to do.

It is said that Shaykh Nur al-Din "the Seer" (may his tomb
be blessed), who was called "the Fourteenth Axis of the
World"[105] and was one of the "forty bodies" upon which the
world stands, was just like my grandfather. That is to say is that
he too was blind and his blessed face was featureless, yet he was
able to do anything that seeing people could do. His pure, luminous tomb is inside the citadel of Samarqand; the mausoleum is
covered with white tilework. The mausoleum had fallen into
disrepair, when Aq Khanum, the wife of Sultan Sa'id Khan, had
it repaired during the governorship of Javanmard 'Ali Khan.
Shaykh Nur al-Din was a very great man. Most of the "forty"
are buried in a mosque known as the Azure Mosque. It is said
that one day in that mosque while a group of sufis were reciting
zikr,[106] the roof of the mosque flew up to the sky and then came
back down again in its place.

Shaykh Nur al-Din had a sufi lodge built outside the Samarqand citadel which is still there. Every Thursday night in that
lodge sufis and well-wishers stay awake all night chanting *zikr*.
The Shaykh had instructed that these "wakeful nights" should
take place there until the Day of Resurrection. People say the
Day of Resurrection will take place on a Friday, at a time when
no one is awake. The Shaykh said, "Almighty God will send
down his angels to ensure that this duty [i.e., all-night vigils] is
carried out."

I myself once took part in such a vigil at that lodge. The
Shaykh's sons got up to chant with the group; people were
whirling around and clapping rhythmically and stamping their

---

[105]The *qutb,* or "axis of the world", was believed to be the best
Muslim alive at any given time. See *Encyclopaedia of Islam* (second
edition), "Ḳutb".

[106]A mantra-like chanting ritual used by sufis, in which various names
of God are "remembered". See *EI2*, "Dhikr".

feet while they chanted. Near dawn they cooked sweets, and after morning prayers they ate *harisa*[107] while standing up.

They say someone once tried to test the Shaykh by throwing a needle on the ground and pretending to look for it. The Shaykh asked him what he was looking for. "I've lost a needle and am looking for it," the man replied. The Shaykh picked up his cane and placed it upon the needle, and said, "Here is your needle, underneath my cane."

Here are some of the Shaykh's quatrains:

> Go, close your eye, that your heart becomes your eye
> With this eye you will see another world
> If you focus the eye of the heart on remembrance of God
> You will see whatever is on the roof of the heavens

> We are like white falcons always on the hunt
> We're all intimate friends with our desires (lit., "lower selves")
> Tomorrow when the curtain is lifted
> We'll know what we all have done

> O heart! You have not obeyed God for an instant
> And you didn't repent of your sin
> You became a sufi, a market controller, and a scholar
> You became all this, but not a Muslim

---

[107] A sort of porridge with meat.

Fourteenth Meeting: A Eulogy to 'Abd al-Rahim Juybari

An evening like the light-giving day of Fortune
From it, Divine Grace was found

When I had come to wait upon His Majesty, he asked, "Who is better, His Excellency 'Abd al-Rahim Khwaja Juybari, or Ilchi Khwaja, Nazr Muhammad Khan's ambassador who is known as Shah Khwaja?"

"Do you mean in terms of noble lineage, or in terms of status and wealth?" I replied.

"I mean in terms of prestige and wealth," he said.

"If you mean in terms of prestige," I said, "there are a hundred *khwaja*s like Ilchi; they get their reward from the generosity of 'Abd al-Rahim Khwaja."

"Bravo!" he said. "Bless you for your fairness. We too have heard just the same thing; this only confirms it. That being the case, could you compose a eulogy in his praise?"

I replied, "I have composed this Arabic eulogy in honor of him:

A Caller called with a perfect voice
From the Divine Throne to Khwaja 'Abd al-Rahim
Blessed be the one who hears
That call with a righteous heart
Yours is the power, the glory and honor
Upon you be the favor of Allah
Meeting you makes wishes come true
Your speech is the triumph of Allah's word
Your breath has messianic qualities
Its words give life to decayed bones
By Allah, the toxic winds have been made

By the influence of your grace a pleasant breeze
In the womb of the Age none like you had been conceived
Your life is the blood of barren mothers
People count your graces upon them
Enclosed within the Eye of Mercy
Hearts always accept you
Thus your moral character is sound
Tribes are enveloped in your graces
Be they the tribe of Salim or of Tamim
I am your servant, by the name of Mutribi
Poor and humble, a stranger and an orphan
I have been the servant of your servants
Forever, and ever, and ever, and ever
O soul, don't despair of your sins
For indeed, blessing comes from the Divine Wellspring
The prayer of the wounded[108] is the final word
The final word is the prayer of the wounded
May the shadows of kindness until the Resurrection
Be ever upon the heads of your devotees.

"Well recited!" said the Emperor.

O God, as long as the Sun and Moon shall be
May Jahangir son of Akbar remain King.

---

[108] Perhaps the reference is to 'Abd al-Rahim's father Khwaja Kalan, whose nickname was "the Wounded".

Fifteenth Meeting: The Origin of Music

Another night the glittering sphere
Arranged the lights of the stars

I arrived at the pedestal of the Heaven-Turning Peerless King and offered my submission and stood at attention. His Highness said,

"Yesterday that sweet-voiced nightingale Fasih Khan let us know of your musical talents. We were talking about our uncle Prince Muhammad Hakim,[109] and what a master of learned expression and the musical arts he was, when the Preacher [i.e., Mutribi] pointed out a few things about him. From that we understood that the Preacher too is a master of these arts, and that this was the meaning of his nickname 'the Minstrel'. If you would share a bit of this skill with those present, be it in the form of painting or crafts, speech, singing, or playing, our servants would be the better for it."

"O Qibla of the World," I replied, "the meaning of my nickname has to do with singing. However, since due to the deficiencies of age my voice has gone, it wouldn't be very pleasant."

"Perfection in singing wears the garb of a defective voice," he said.

So a drum was brought out; I took it and asked, "What song should I sing, and in what style?"

"I always used to hear the old styles at family gatherings," he said. "But now I would really like to hear something in the

---

[109]Emperor Akbar's brother (b.1554). He was governor of Kabul until his death in 1585 at the age of 31.

style of Master 'Ali Dust the *nay* player from the time of 'Abdullah Khan Uzbek. If you know it, sing some."

I sang a *sawt al-'amali* by Ustad 'Ali composed in the *'iraq* mode (*ahang*), in the rhythm cycle (*usul*) *nim saqil*, with a change of rhythm in the ritornello (*bazgui*), whose opening section is in *'iraq*, whose middle section is in *husayni*, whose ritornello is in *'uzzal*, and whose refrain contains a *mustahal*.

I sang.

"Bravo," the Emperor said when I had finished this *'amal*. "You sang it nicely. The beat and articulation were both good, and they didn't diverge from each other.

Then I sang a *naqsh* by the aforementioned master, in the *sigah* mode using the *dar-shahi* rhythm, in the style of the *naqsh* "*naz u niyaz*" by Sultan Husayn and Amir 'Ali-Shir[110], which is composed in the *husayni* mode and *turki-darb* rhythm, and a *sawt* by the aforementioned master, composed in the *nishavarak* mode for 'Abdullah Khan in the *far'* rhythm.

"We won't trouble you any further," said the Emperor. Then he asked, "What are the sources of the twelve modes?"

"There is some disagreement about it," I replied. "What I have read in the treatises of Mawlana Hasan 'the Celestial' and Khwaja Kalan 'the Wounded' is that according to Pythagoras the derivation is from the twelve signs of the zodiac, because every day the heavens pass through each house and make a sound, and the sound of each house is one of the modes. This is elaborated and made clear in those treatises.

"However, according to Mir 'Atallah al-Husayni and some of the ancients, the source is from the holes in the beak of the Phoenix, the story of which is detailed in the verses of the book, *The Logic of the Birds*, which was written as a treatise on alchemy by Shaykh Farid al-Din 'Attar.[111] As the Shaykh explains in this couplet:

---

[110] Nava`i, who along with Jami was one of the two famous poets at the court of Sultan Husayn. He is considered the greatest poet of the Chaghatay Turkish language.

[111]In the twelfth century mystic's account, the phoenix has a long beak pierced with holes like a flute (Farid al-Din 'Attar, *The Conference of*

'There was a philosopher who became his companion
And learned the art of music from his song'.

"But the most likely explanation is what Makhdumi Hasan
Khwaja Nisari wrote in his book *Remembrance of Friends*, that
when Moses (peace be upon him) was wandering around for
forty days and nights in the desert with the tribe of Israel and
praying to Bala'am son of Ba'u[112], one day due to the lack of
water and their overwhelming thirst the people of Israel were
beseeching Moses (peace be upon him) to do something; he in
turn sought help from God Almighty. The proclamation came
from the Lord of lords, 'O Moses! Strike the stone with your
walking stick!'[113] Moses carried out the command of the Nour-
isher of Creation and struck the stone with his cane. Immediately, as it says in the noble verse, 'And out of it came twelve
wellsprings'[114], twelve springs of water flowed out from the
rock.

"The people of Israel were made up of twelve tribes; each
tribe was assigned a spring of water, and from each spring water
flowed making a tune. From Almighty God came the command,

---

the Birds, tr. Afkhami Darbandi and Dick Davis, London: Penguin,
1984, 116).

[112]Balaam son of Beor, a Mesopotamian diviner summoned by the
king of Moab to curse the Israelites (see Numbers 22-24). Two biblical
stories are confounded here.

[113]Qur'an 2: 60; cf. Exodus 17:1-7, Numbers 20: 3-12.

[114]Ibid.

'*Ya Musa, qiyy!*'[115] That is, 'O Moses, memorize this song!' That is why the art has come to be called 'music' (*musiqi*)."

"Perhaps," said the Divine Viceregent, "this art is derived from *all* these sources."

I replied,

> O God, as long as the Sun and Moon shall be
> May Jahangir son of Akbar remain King.

---

[115]Lit., "O Moses, keep (memorise this)!" This is an amusing, and clearly fallacious, popular etymology.

Sixteenth Meeting: The Piety of a Slave

A night like the truthful morning, spreading light
Heart and soul illuminated by its light

I had the good fortune of approaching the foot of the throne adorned by the presence of the Divine Viceregent. He said, "We sometimes make lawful use of slaves, in accordance with the Qur'anic verse regarding buying and selling, 'Then rejoice in the bargain which you have concluded'[116]." Then three slave boys were brought out, and he continued, "We bought these. Now we're going to sell them. Is there anyone present who would like to buy them from us?"

The sweet-voiced nightingale Fasih Khan, who is His Majesty's alchemist, said, "I'll take one slave. Let a price for him be set." A slave-merchant set his price at two hundred rupees. Fasih Khan accepted this price and bought the slave boy. Another of the slave boys, who was younger, was bought by an intimate of the Court by the name of Muhammad Husayn Khalaf. One slave boy was left.

My son Muhammad 'Ali was present. He said, "I will buy this slave boy for my father for the purpose of bringing ablution water and preparing the prayer-place; let a price be set for him."

His Majesty said, "The price of this slave boy is one hundred and twenty rupees."

"O Qibla of the World!" my son replied, "I have only one hundred rupees."

"I just gave your father a thousand rupees," said the Emperor. "Where did that money go?"

---

[116]Qur'an, 9: 111. Jahangir has taken the verse out of context; it does not encourage traffic in slaves.

One of the intimates of the Court said, "Maybe they sent it back home."

My son then accepted the slave for the stipulated sum. When we got back to our lodgings we realized the slave boy was deaf; he didn't respond to our words. We were dismayed by the realization that returning the slave boy to His Majesty would be impossible.

The next day I counted out one hundred twenty rupees and put them in a purse, and came to kiss the royal threshold. Although grandees of the State and His Majesty's nobles such as Navvab Asaf Khan, Khwaja Abu'l-Hasan Tarbati[117], Khavvas Khan, Iradat Khan, and Doctor Masih al-Zaman were present, His Majesty's enlightened gaze fell upon this humble servant. He said, "Preacher! What have you got in your hand?"

"I brought the money for the slave-boy," I replied.

"Isn't that slave-boy of yours deaf?" he asked.

"O Qibla of the World," I said, "he's as deaf as can be."

The word was spread about the assembly. The Emperor said, "I'm giving you the price of the slave-boy, and adding a hundred rupees."

I bowed and said,

"O God, as long as the Sun and Moon shall be
May Jahangir on of Akbar remain King".

That slave-boy is still in my service. He brings my ablution water and towel and prepares the prayer-place, and carries out all the required duties of service. He is an exemplary model of piety and asceticism. It may be hoped that because of his abilities he will rise to the station of the Perfected Ones[118], as other slaves by their pious and agreeable qualities have done.

In Samarqand near the Basket Bazaar, on an upper floor there was a slave. Day and night he would go around the streets and bazaars crying out "God! God!" in a loud voice. On returning home he wouldn't sleep, but would carry out the duties of

---

[117]He is the Abu'l Hasan-i Divan mentioned earlier.

[118]This is sufi terminology.

the soul. Sometimes he would come to the house of the Chief
Justice Saqi Ramini. The judge would bow before him.
One day that slave was passing before a school. A child was
reciting from the works of Amir Qasim Anvar; he stopped and
listened to him for an hour, and when the child came to the following couplet:

> "Those who look anywhere but at your face
> Are short of sight— and how short of sight"

He let out a sigh and fell to the ground, and gave up the ghost.

In connection with this, one day the Learned One of the Age
Maktub Khan repeated the following story. The Divine Viceregent was visiting one of the provinces of India. Sweet-voiced
qawwali singers were singing songs. One of these talented singers sang the following hemistich of Shaykh Nizam al-Din
Awliya[119]:

> "Every righteous nation is religious and qibla-directed".

The second hemistich is from Khwaja Khusraw Dihlawi[120]:

> "We found the true qibla towards the quarter of the one who
> has his turban awry"[121].

When this couplet was sung, one of the servants of the Divine
Viceregent, a man named Ahmad 'Ali Mihr Kun, heard it, then
let out a sigh and went cold in his place. By the time they at-
tended to him, his soul had gone to meet God. I have seen this

---

[119]A fourteenth century sufi saint of the Chishti order; his shrine at
Dehli continues to attract many visitors. This verse, however, is not by
him, but by one of his disciples.

[120]Amir Khusraw, a great fourteenth century poet and musician,
credited with introducing the sitar to India.

[121]Certain sufi groups would tie their turbans slightly to one side as a
mark of identity. The expression "*kaj-kolah*" also means "coquettish."

incident written about in the *Book of Jahangir*,[122] which is the
sound work of His Majesty, and described it again here.

---

[122]*Tuzuk-i Jahangiri*, i, 169-70.

Seventeenth Meeting: Trading Verses

Another day, illuminated by the Sun of the resplendent heavens
Benefit comes from prostration upon the dust of the path of the King

I had the good fortune to kiss the ground in submission before the Fortunate Throne of the Auspicious King. He said, "The sweet-voiced nightingale [Fasih Khan] has been reading your book to us every day for hours. We enjoy it very much. Today couplets by Khwaja Husayn "Sadr" and "Miram Siah" were heard which were very, very well written. Recite those two couplets for us."

I recited them:

"Cup-bearer, bring the purple wine around the garden;
Know the value of spring and life and days of youth".

Then "Miram Siah":

From that day when I gave up the purple wine
I have never seen good times or happiness".

"Miram Siah," however, is from Khurasan, and is known for talking nonsense. Since no one pays attention to his gibberish, nothing has been written about it. But some people think it is because he is close to God, and say that divine inspiration is such that not everyone can unveil its secrets.

It is said that one day he appeared at a festive gathering given by the Guardian of Truth and Seal of Auspiciousness (may he be sanctified)[123], and His Excellency Makhdumi[124] asked him to recite an ode. He recited the following:

> Companionship with a beautiful idol is a boon; raise the cup
> of the paradisiacal fountain
> No one is guarantor for the funds of life
> Don't be greedy, so that you become the one dear to the world
> I have seen many respected ones ruined by such greed
> Fear even the weak enemy and count him as strong
> Even the elephant loses sleep from fear of the mosquito
> If one good person is disloyal to his own clan
> Everywhere a hard-hearted one exists, it is from him
> Miram, take the wine cup from the hands
> Of those with tulip cheeks, and leave the gossip

His Excellency Makhdumi said, "Anyone who can compose poetry like this, it is a shame that he talks nonsense."

Miram replied, "Makhdum! However gracefully I compose poetry, I'll never make it into your circle of disciples. But when I compose poetry, then neither can you enter my circle. And if you can't, then who?"

It is reported that one of the merchants close to Makhdumi (may he be sanctified) came and asked for an ode from the collection of his fragrant mind, that he might take it back to Samarqand for the good luck of the scholars there. Makhdumi told him, "Any ode you could take as a gift would not be better than one of Miram Siah's." So he wrote out one of Miram Siah's and gave it to him.

I was commissioned by one of the sultans of Turan to put that ode into pentastiches. This is it:

> Before setting off on the road of love
> O heart, listen to some advice, don't ask me for an explanation
> In the garden by the edge of the channel,
> Companionship with a beautiful idol is a boon;

---

[123]'Abd al-Rahman Jami, court poet of Sultan Husayn Bayqara.

[124]a.k.a. Khwaja Kasani, first head of the Dihbidi family and spiritual guide to several Shibanid rulers.

Raise the cup of the paradisiacal fountain
No one is guarantor for the funds of life

How long in the world of sorrows old and new
Will you seek sustenance in every corner?
How long out of greed will you follow nobodies?
Don't be greedy, so that you become the one dear to the world
I have seen many respected ones ruined by such greed

O you who have power for a time
And are seeking your heart's desire
Listen to this point from the wise (lit., "sober"):
Fear even the weak enemy and count him as strong
Even the elephant loses sleep from fear of the mosquito

The pains of my heart for which the beloved had no remedy
Had no mercy on my wretched affliction
This world, O heart, makes no mistake
If one good person is disloyal to his own clan
Everywhere a hard-hearted one exists, it is from him

O Mutribi, once you sobered up
You had no more desire for gardens and meadows
Our heart now bears a thousand scars
Miram, take the wine cup from the hands
Of those with tulip cheeks, and leave the gossip.

His Majesty said, "Don't forget that response to another of
Miram Siah's odes:

'I don't lose the desire for the days of youth
When in old age I lose my head drinking purple wine.'"

Upon his command I too composed the following:

He finds in this world life everlasting
Who drinks purple wine from the royal palm
He finds in this world paradise everlasting
Who takes purple wine from the palm of coquettish youth.

Several of the servants of the Divine Viceregent composed responses to these odes. After listening to them His Majesty recited:

> "Don't stop drinking in old age
> That in old age you'll find the desire for youth."

That same day I was again by the foot of the great throne. That day ten bags, each bag filled with a thousand rupees, were given to the Doctor [Masih al-Zaman]. I didn't know whether this was a prize for his couplet, or for some medical treatment that had been useful in treating some illness. The reward was given; God knows best.

Doctor Masih al-Zaman is one of the intimates of the foot of the World-Turning Throne of the Divine Viceregent. He is extremely good-natured; His Majesty trusts his word completely, and gave him a nice mention in the *Book of Jahangir*, where he says, "When the World-Axis of the Age, His Excellency Khwaja Abu Hashim Dihbidi— whose blessed breath today warms the bazaar of asceticism in Transoxiana— sent us presents by means of his disciples, in return we sent him a piece written by Babur for his grandfather Makhdum-i A'zam (may he be sanctified):

> We have wasted our life following our lower self
> Before God's devotees we're ashamed of our ways
> Cast a glance our way, for we with turning heads
> Have lacked mastery, and are slaves of the Master.

"We gave a thousand jahangiri *muhr*s to his disciples, and in a letter to him I wrote this verse:

> Whose kindness towards me is boundless
> For you I'll renounce all worldy goods
> So joyful is my heart made by news of you
> Joyful from your boundless favor.[125]

"The point is," he continued, "that whatever has the quality of poetry is in response to this quatrain. There have been many

---

[125]On this incident cf. *Tuzuk*, i, 303-4.

responses, but I liked that of Doctor Masih al-Zaman and gave him the prize of jahangiri *muhrs*. This is Masih al-Zaman's quatrain:

> 'Even if we have royal business before us
> We remember the former dervishes every second
> When an ascetic is pleased with us
> We count it as our own royal harvest'".

Another day I heard that the Learned One of the Age Maktub Khan too had composed a response to Miram Siah's ode but didn't present it, because on the day when he wanted to come and present it to the Divine Viceregent he tripped and broke his arm. When I went to visit him, he composed these three couplets and gave them to me:

> In penitance, since I dropped the cup
> The penalty for this sin was that my hand be broken
> Now I break my repentance of the cup of wine
> Had I not lost the use of my penitent hand
> I hope of King Jahangir
> That he'll intoxicate me once again with his glance.

This humble servant added the following:

> Is not the sea of Maktub Khan's qualities
> From the tyranny of the sky, even if his hand is broken?
> Don't be broken-hearted for God's sake
> For in every brokenness there is righteousness.

He gave me an offering[126] of fine cloth along with five hundred rupees and his apologies. He also composed this couplet with the same intention:

> The fault for our not coming to attend on you
> Is that of a broken hand, tied to a wooden splint.

---

[126]Lit., *tüqqüz*, the Turkish word for nine, since by tradition one had to offer gifts to the Mughal emperors by nines.

Then he wrote down his response to Miram Siah's ode:

> For the King's sake I drink purple wine from the royal cup
> So that in old age I might remember youth
> Communicate in silence with the rose
> Even though the nightingale doesn't know that language
> What enjoyment is there in the life of eternal Khizr[127]
> If life doesn't make use of companionship?
> For the friends of the King, I ask God's mercy
> For his enemies, sudden calamity
> In old age 'Farsi' drinks of this purple wine
> Since the days of youth were spent in the company of the King.

---

[127]A mythical figure representing eternal life, associated with the prophet Elijah (Gk. Elias), who had drunk from the water of life. See Qur'an 18: 65 ff.

Eighteenth Meeting: Correcting Portraits, and An Impertinence

Another day the world received the turn of fortune
The golden idol got silver balls, the shrub wings

I came to kiss the threshold. The Emperor had a miniature painting in his hand and was studying it. He called me forward, and told me,

"Look at this painting. Do you know whose portrait it is?"

When I looked I saw that one was a portrait of 'Abdullah Khan Uzbek and another was of 'Abd al-Mu'min Khan[128].

"Are these good likenesses," he asked me, "or do you have some comments to make? If you do, then tell me."

"The portrait of 'Abdullah Khan is too fleshy, and his chin was not as straight as it's shown here," I replied. "In fact he was rather thin, and he had a crooked chin."

"Was it crooked on the right side, or the left?" he asked.

"On the left," I said.

A painter was called out to correct the portrait, and whatever I said he was ordered to make the appropriate changes. Then the Emperor asked, "What about the portrait of 'Abd al-Mu'min Khan?"

"He's painted very greenish here," I said. "He wasn't like that; in fact he was more white than green, and he wore his turban a little more to the front, as neatly as possible."

"Take off your turban," he said, "and show me how he did it."

---

[128] 'Abdullah Khan's successor, the last of the Shibanid dynasty. He ruled from 1598-1599.

I took off my turban and showed him. The Emperor said to the painter, "Paint it this way."

The next day the painter brought out the paintings just the way I had said they should be. His Majesty was very pleased. Abu'l Biy Uzbek, who is known as Bahadur Khan, was present, and said, "During the time I was in 'Abd al-Mu'min's service he didn't tie his turban like that."

The Divine Viceregent replied, "The Preacher was talking about when he was still a prince, which was almost fifty years ago."

Then he asked me, "Did 'Abd al-Mu'min Khan compose poetry?"

"Yes," I replied.

"Recite some," he said. Accordingly, I recited this:

> "May my heart be cut to pieces by a double-edged sword
> If one day I should be without your love."

One of the attendants said, "'Abd al-Mu'min Khan composed a stupid couplet."

The Divine Viceregent replied, "Even if 'Abd al-Mu'min Khan composed a stupid couplet, your interruption is even stupider." What he meant was that one has no right to point out the faults of kings, especially their words, since "the most kingly words are the words of kings".[129]

O dear brother! And O friend of the Pure Master! Be very, very careful to watch over your eye and tongue and hand, and be careful, for many, for lack of watching over these things, have given their souls to the wind. Above all, the most important is to keep watch over your tongue.

> When they strike the sword at life
> They are really striking at the tongue

---

[129]Ar. *Muluk al-kalam kalam al-muluk.*

And that is why tongue (*zaban*) rhymes with loss (*ziyan*).

Nineteenth Meeting: Khwaja Juybari

Another day that I arrived at the tent[130] of the King
I found sanctuary in its shelter

The Emperor said, "Praise be to Allah, we have been honored with the visit of the great and luminous Khawja ʿAbd al-Rahim Juybari. We hope that we will also be honored with a visit from his blessed brother Taj al-Din Hasan[131]."

Then to me he said, "Do you have any stories you can tell us about their noble qualities?"

"Your health, O Qibla of the World," I replied; "Everything you have borne witness to regarding the nobility of ʿAbd al-Rahim Khwaja, I think exactly the same."

"I will express it even more strongly," said the Emperor, "because he is like an elder brother to me.

"On the other hand," he continued, "we didn't hold His Excellency ʿAbdi Khwaja[132] in such high regard as we do His Excellency ʿAbd al-Rahim Khwaja. So if we should be having a conversation with him, keep this in mind."

---

[130]While traveling or on campaign the Mughal Emperors, recalling their Turko-Mongol origins, set up court in lavish tents.

[131]He was the head of the family, being the eldest of the three brothers.

[132]ʿAbd al-Rahim's younger brother, who had been in Mughal service prior to his death in 1607.

I replied,

> "O God, as long as the Sun and Moon shall be
> May Jahangir son of Akbar remain King."

Twentieth Meeting: More Central Asian Acquaintances

Another evening that the Just Emperor
Took his place upon the Throne of Fortune

I had the good fortune to be received at the foot of the throne. The Emperor said,

"We were very carefully reading your anthology today, when your mention of Muhammad Yusuf Khwaja son of Taj al-Din Hasan Juybari[133] fell under our enlightened gaze. Having read one of his odes, we realized that he is very talented and composes very nice poetry. Even though he was known to us even before Khwaja Zayn al-Din Naqshbandi[134] introduced him to us, we didn't know much about his poetry. Now we have understood the extent of his skill, and that of all the Juybari khwajas it appears none are as talented as he.

"We also read your mention of Fawlad Khwaja Shaykh al-Islam," the Emperor continued. "He is certainly a master of high ambition. But what a pity he hasn't come to India and that the light of his erudition has in no way fallen here, and that he hasn't come to give the devotees an apple of Samarqand wisdom.[135] You will pass on our complaint to him.

---

[133]Muhammad Yusuf succeeded Taj al-Din as head of the family on the latter's death in 1646. See Foltz, "Naqshbandi Connections," 239.

[134]*Tuzuk*, i, 289.

[135]Samarqand was famous for the quality of its apples.

"We also hear that Nadr Divan Begi[136] has become an intimate of the ruler of Turan Imam Quli Khan. Is this true or not?"

"Yes," I replied; "he gave evidence for this in an order which he had written out in the name 'Nizam al-Din Nadr Mirza-yi Tughay'."

"I can't believe he is an intimate of Imam Quli Khan," said the Emperor. "Imam Quli Khan never sends his intimates to us as ambassadors, only low-ranking servants and inferior people. That's what we're concerned about. We don't know if this is a good sign or not."[137]

I said,

> "O God, as long as the Son and Moon shall be
> May Jahangir son of Akbar remain King."

---

[136]He was a high official of Turan and a generous patron. A seminary bearing his name still stands on the main square of Bukhara; he also had a *madrasa* built at Khwaja Ahrar's tomb in Samarqand.

[137]Imam Quli had broken off diplomatic relations with Jahangir a number of years earlier, ostensibly a because Jahangir had joked about the Turani ruler's inclinations to pederasty (Muhammad Yusuf b. Khwaja Baqa, *Tazkira-i Muqim Khani*, Russian tr. A.A. Semënov, *Mukimkhanskaya Istoriia*, Tashkent, 1956, 90). Nur Jahan was active in bringing about a reconciliation of sorts between the two rulers. See M. Athar Ali, "Jahangir and the Uzbeks,"*Proceedings of the 26th Indian History Congress*, (1964), 111.

Twenty-First Meeting: Mutribi's Poetic Ages

Another day, that the world received light from the sun
The drunken cup-bearer had another cup of wine

I came to kiss the threshold. The Emperor said, "Fasih Khan has been reading your anthology to us for several hours every day; we very much enjoy hearing it. You wrote about the incident involving Mawlana Nizari Badakhshi very well and your criticisms of him were quite eloquent. If you have this style of discourse in your head, you should put more of it into your book."

Then he asked, "How many years of age has the Preacher reached?"

"I have composed a quatrain from which it can be known how old I am," I replied.

"Then recite it," he said.

I recited it:

"At the end of life, since God gave the fortune
Of opening the road toward the realm of Lahore
The sight of imperial Jahangir was seen
On that day I was seventy".

Some ignoramous interrupted me, adding a final "i" when I pronounced "Jahangir" to make it "jahangiri".[138] His Majesty rebuffed him and said, "It was good the way the Preacher recited it."

Let it not be concealed from the enlightened minds of the illuminating suns of the masters of fidelity that when your

---

[138]That is, he was adding a syllable to correct the meter.

humble servant was nearing the age of "shaykhliness" which is sixty, I made a pledge that subsequently for every year of my life I would compose a quatrain in which my age would be made apparent. So far I have not failed to do this. Hopefully I will reach the natural lifespan (Amen!), just as my great ancestor Malik Arghun did.

These are my quatrains:

> Alas; we've grown old and lost our touch
> Lament that the glory of youth is broken
> The games of the forties and fifties are past
> We've played into the house of sixty[139]

> O Mutribi, today that you've become sixty-one
> You're still preoccupied with your stomach
> It almost happened that I drank poison from the teats of death
> Instead of milk like a baby

> O Mutribi! Come and shorten the tale
> Put an end to all your books òf wishes
> Now you've turned sixty-two
> Don't sit in negligence; get up and set yourself straight

> O Mutribi! You've passed sixty-two
> What has happened to you in that time?
> While you're sixty-three whatever you do
> You can't improve yourself
> Since your best days have passed

> O Mutribi! Your heart is tired, your chest exhausted
> Count the days of the life you have lived
> Until when, you ask; how old am I?
> Since sixty-three has passed, you're sixty-four

> O Mutribi! Don't speak of possessions or of hopes
> Opportunity is a boon; speak the truth now
> A hundred thanks for the days of life
> You've become sixty-five this year

---

[139]A technical term from backgammon.

When I became sixty-five, throughout the next year I was ill to the point of death. Since in my sixty-sixth year God Almighty gave me a reprieve, I composed the following couplet:

> Since I passed the age of sixty-five
> Weakness and suffering have passed
> I'm sixty-six now and out of mercy
> That exquisite Friend put off my detractors
>
> O Mutribi! How long will you think of this world?
> How long will you think of these trivialities and enigmas?
> Your feet are stuck in the house of sixty-seven
> How long will you busy yourself with bad deeds and good?
>
> O Mutribi! This year that you've gone traveling
> I passed by chance through Balkh
> I saw myself in the country of sixty-eight
> Every day in another station, and at night someplace else
>
> We flew like the wind from Balkh homeward
> We were gladdened by the sight of our friends
> Dear life has arrived at sixty-nine
> Negligent until when? We're heading towards seventy

The quatrain for seventy years has already been written. This is the quatrain for seventy-one:

> A hundred thanks that by the kindness of God the Gracious
> I went towards Lahore like the wind across a meadow
> During the journey I turned seventy
> At seventy-one, I arrived home again.

Twenty-Second Meeting: A Commitment to Timur's Tomb

Another day that King of kings Jahangir of the heavens
Showed his face in the mirror of a turquoise angel

I arrived at the happiness of kissing the threshold. The pleasantness of Samarqand was being discussed. The Emperor asked me, "Is Samarqand spelled with a 'q' or with a 'k'?"

"Either way is correct," I replied. "In Tabari's history and several other books it is referred to as Samarkand, but in popular usage it has become known as Samarqand. Some say that the name comes from Samar and Qamar, two slaves of Alexander the great who built the city which was then named for them.[140] Their graves are situated in the main market square of Samarqand."

The Divine Viceregent said, "We've also seen it spelled Samarkand in books." Then he asked, "Do you know anyone in Samarqand erudite and articulate and good-natured and companionable enough to be deserving of our royal company, that we might send them money and an invitation?"

My son Muhammad 'Ali then greatly praised Akhund Mawlana Sabiri, son of Hafiz Tashkandi[141] who is also known as Hafiz "the Celestial", and brought him to the attention of His Majesty. The Divine Viceregent said, when we were nine years old we often saw his father conversing with our own great father; he was the best sort of person."

---

[140]Actually the city was already flourishing in Alexander's time; it appears in Arrian as Maracanda.

[141]*A'in-i Akbari*, i, 540; *Tabaqat-i Akbari*, ii, 686.

Then he said, "The shrine of our great honored ancestors, which is known as the *Gur-i Amir*, how many rupees does its maintenance cost?"

"If you want to do it properly, 10,000 rupees," I said; "otherwise 5,000 rupees just to keep it going."

"If 10,000 rupees will maintain it," he said, "then we have decided that in accordance with your information we will send 10,000 rupees, in order that that blessed station be maintained."[142]

I said,

> "O God, as long as the Sun and the Moon shall be
> May Jahangir son of Akbar remain King."

---

[142]Cf. *Tuzuk-i Jahangiri*, ii, 196.

Twenty-Third Meeting: A Royal Commission

Another day, that my heart set out towards the King
My lips kissed the dust of the royal path

Following the auspiciousness of threshold-kissing the Emperor showed me his favor and said, "Preacher, today Fasih Khan finished reading us your anthology. I sent that enjoyable work— 'Like unto rubies and coral'[143]— to Maktub Khan so that he might add it to our personal library and look after it with special care.

"Furthermore it occurred to our enlightened mind that your *Book of Jahangir* would be a nice complement to our own anthology. At the time of our princehood, we gathered several pages of names of poets who existed in the royal days of our great father (God have mercy on him). Since this was very brief, we saw it would be fitting to have it included within your anthology. You could then have the blessing of bringing to this work the garb of completion, and that would be very nice."

I bowed and said,

"O God, as long as the Sun and Moon shall be
May Jahangir son of Akbar remain King."

---

[143]Qur'an, 55: 58.

Twenty-Fourth Meeting: Permission to Return Home

> Another day lit by the sun; permission was given
> Toward the center of fortune with a hundred blessings haste
> was made

I came to attend on the Divine Viceregent. From several of the grandees of the State and His Majesty's officials I heard that His majesty was busy assigning positions and distributing rupees and other gifts. This was because all the royal servants were going to leave town, and accompany the Emperor to Kashmir.

This being understood, I would have liked to commit the remainder of my life to the service of the Divine Viceregent.

> We and service to you; if that was life
> Fortunate is he who is in your service

But because of homesickness— in accordance with the saying "Love of one's land is an act of faith"[144]— it was not possible to do this. Moreover things like old age and senility and weaknesses due to old age prevented going into such service. I've been troubled with colds, coughing, sneezing and yawning, and since during royal gatherings His Highness forbade these things, the heart was more inclined to ask permission to return home. This being the case, I sought advice from the book of Shaykh Farid al-Din 'Attar, and came upon this couplet:

> "Therefore don't get too close to kings
> And if you do get close to them, keep your distance".

---

[144]Ar. *Hubb al-watan min al-iman.*

Know this, my friend! Even if service to kings is very profitable, it can put your life in danger, since "the loyal ones are most important."[145], and for that reason the wise have said that service to kings is like an ocean voyage:

> Merchants start with money in both hands at the store
> Or one day a wave casts them on shore, dead.

Some people, mindful of the Qur'anic verse, "And make not your hands contribute to your destruction"[146], employ themselves in well-wishing for kings from afar. Others throw their hearts and souls into danger and remain day and night in visible proximity around kings. This humble servant, therefore, was caught between these two extremes, when the divine inspiration came to me that the proper course would be to ask permission to return home and not keep my children and relatives blindly waiting.

Therefore, having extemporized the following ode in the company of the grandees of the State and His Majesty's nobles, I presented it to the Divine Viceregent:

> "The eye which looks elsewhere than at your face
> That eye is then deserving of the sword
> Your quarter is the Ka'aba—who enters it is safe[147]
> The door of His mercy is open to every heart
> I'm happy that my forehead has reached the station of my heart
> For there, near and far are the same
> The heart is again set towards home, Mutribi
> If only Jahangir son of Akbar gives permission".

When this ode was heard by the Court, everyone was speechless. Asaf Khan said, "By the Qibla of the Worlds! What is Preacher Mutribi saying?"

---

[145] Ar. *Al-mukhlisun 'ala khatar 'adhimun.*
[146] Qur'an, 2: 195.
[147] Ar. *Man dakhala kana amanan.*

His Majesty made a face and said angrily, "What do you mean? He wants permission to go."

Then he calmed down and turned to me, and said, "Preacher, your ode was appropriately done, and we accept it. But we just thought up a couplet on the same subject and in the same rhyme and meter as your ode. It would be appropriate for you to incorporate it into your ode."

I bowed, and said,

> "O God, as long as the Sun and Moon shall be
> May Jahangir son of Akbar remain King."

Then with his own blessed speech he recited:

> "Turn your face from me, for I can't be an instant without you
> One broken heart from you is equal to a hundred deaths".

Then he asked me, "Where is it that you want permission to go?"

"I will go to Samarqand," I replied.

"Why do you wish to go?" he asked.

"I have unfinished business," I said. "I will convey your gifts to the spiritual masters there, so that they will be among your well-wishers."

"How many dependents do you have?" he asked me.

"Twenty people," I answered.

"You come to the paradise of Kashmir with us," he said, "and we will send two thousand rupees to Samarqand to bring your dependents to you."

I continued to beg for permission to leave. His Majesty became discomfited and said,

"You really want us to give you permission. We have never seen such an insistent person!"

Then he placed his Justice-Worshipping hand upon his ungrudging chest, looking like a portrait, and said, "We have given permission, on the condition that you promise to return to the World-Protecting Court once again within the course of one year."

I bowed, recited the Fatiha, then went out and offered a prayer of thanks; "And peace to all who follow guidance"[148]. In conclusion, I composed this double-rhyme quatrain:

A hundred thanks that this book has been completed
And that our book from its beginning has reached its end
The image to which Mutribi aspired in this world
Has emerged from behind the curtain of the days

Thanks be to God that this book was finished
Before life came to an end.

---

[148]Qur'an, 20: 47. According to hadith accounts Muhammad would end his invitations to the kings of the world to accept Islam with this phrase. The Ayatullah Khumayni, likewise, used to end his letters to Saddam Husayn thus.

Bibliography

Abu'l Fazl 'Allami, *Akbar-nama*, tr. H. Beveridge, 3 vols., Calcutta: Royal Asiatic Society of Bengal, 1902-39. *A'in-i Akbari*, tr. Henry Blochmann (v. 1) and H.S. Jarrett (vols. 2 and 3), Bibliotheca Indica, Calcutta: Royal Asiatic Society of Bengal, 1877-96 (rev. Phillott and Sarkar, reprint Oriental Books Reprint Corporation, Delhi, 1977-78).

Ahmedov, Buri A., *Istoriko-geograficheskaia literatura Srednei Azii XVI-XVIII vv.*, Tashkent: Fan, 1985. "Tazkira Mutribi kak istochnik po istorii i kul'ture XVI-XVII vv.", *Istochnikovedenie i Tekstologiia srednevekogo Blizhnego i Srednego Vostoka*, Moscow: Nauka, 1984, 36-44.

Ali, M. Athar, *Apparatus of Empire: Awards of Ranks, Offices and Titles to the Mughal Nobility (1574-1658)*, Delhi: Oxford University Press, 1985. "Jahangir and the Uzbeks," *Proceedings of the 26th Indian History Congress*, (1964), 108-119.

'Attar, Farid al-din, *The Conference of the Birds*, tr. Afkhami Darbandi and Dick Davis, London: Penguin, 1984.

Babur, Zahir al-din Muhammad, *The Babur-nama*, translated by W.M. Thackston, Jr., Washington: Smithsonian and New York and Oxford: Oxford University Press, 1996; Annette S. Beveridge, tr., *The Babur-nama in English*, London, 1921.

Banks, Findlay Ellison, *Nur Jahan*, New York: Oxford University Press, 1996.

Barthold, V.V., *Turkestan Down to the Mongol Invasion*, London: Luzac, 1977.

Ethé, Hermann, *Catalogue of Persian Manuscripts in the India Office Library*, Oxford, 1937.

Foltz, Richard, *Mughal India and Central Asia*, Karachi: Oxford University Press,1998.
"Two Seventeenth Century Central Asian Travelers to Mughal India", *Journal of the Royal Asiatic Society*, ser. 3, 6/3 (1996), 367-377.
"The Central Asian Naqshbandi Connections of the Mughal Emperors", *Journal of Islamic Studies* 7/2 (1996), 229-239.
'The Mughal Occupation of Balkh, 1646-1647", *Journal of Islamic Studies* 7/1 (1996), 49-61.

Gulbadan Begum, *Humayun-nama*, tr. Annette S. Beveridge, London: Royal Asiatic Society, 1902 (reprint Lahore, 1987).

Gulchin-Ma'ani, Ahmad, *Karvan-i Hind*, 2 vols., Mashhad: Astan-i Quds-i Razavi, 1370 (1990-91).

Guldasta-yi Samarqand, Tashkent: Gafur Ghulom and Dushanbe: Adib, 1989.

Hasan Nisari, *Muzakkir-i Ahbab*, Hyderabad, Pakistan, 1969. Uzbek version Tashkent, 1993.

Inayat Khan, *Shah Jahan-nama*, tr. A.R. Fuller, ed. W.E. Begley and Z.A. Desai, Delhi: Oxford University Press, 1990.

Islam, Riazul, *A Calendar of Documents on Indo-Persian Relations (1500-1750)*, 2 vols., Tehran: Iranian Culture Foundation, and Karachi: Institute of Central and West Asian Studies, 1979-82.

Jahangir, Nur al-din Muhammad, *Tuzuk-i Jahangiri*, tr. A. Rogers, ed. H. Beveridge, 2 vols., Bibliotheca Indica, Calcutta,

1909-14 (single volume reprint New Delhi: Munshiram Mano-harlal, 1978); new translation by Wheeler Thackston forthcoming 1998.

Kumar, Anil, *Asaf Khan and His Times*, Patna, 1986.

Lal, Muni, *Jahangir*, Delhi: Vikas, 1983.

McChesney, R.D., "The Anthology of Poets: Muzakkir al-Ashab as a source for the history of 17th century Central Asia", in *Intellectual Studies on Islam*, eds. M. Mazzaoui and Moreen, Salt Lake City: University of Utah Press, 1990, 57-84.

Mirzoev, Abdul-Ghani, ed., *Khatirat-i Mutribi Samarqandi*, Karachi: Institute of Central and West Asian Studies, 1977.
Nuskha-yi Ziba-yi Jahangiri, Karachi: Institute of Central and West Asian Studies, 1976.

Muhammad Yusuf b. Khwaja Baqa, *Tazkira-i Muqim Khani*, Russian tr. A.A. Semёnov, *Mukimkhanskaya Istoriia*, Tashkent, 1956.

"Mutribi" al-Asamm Samarqandi, *Tazkira al-Shu'ara*, Institute of Oriental Studies, Uzbekistan Academy of Sciences, MS no. 2253.
Tarikh-i Jahangiri, India Office Library, MS no. 3023.

Nizam al-Din Ahmad, *Tabaqat-i Akbari*, tr. B. De, 3 vols., Bibliotheca Indica, Calcutta, 1911-41.

Nizamutdinov, Ilyas G., *Ocherki istorii kul'turnykh sviazei Srednei Azii i Indii v XVI- nachalie XX vv.*, Tashkent: Fan, 1981.
Iz istorii Sredneaziatsko-Indiiskikh otnoshenii, Tashkent: Uzbekistan, 1969.

Pant, Chandra, *Nur Jahan and Her Family*, Allahabad: Dandewal, 1978.

Prasad, Beni, *History of Jahangir*, Allahabad: Indian Press, 1940.

Richards, John F., *The Mughal Empire*, The New Cambridge History of India, Cambridge: Cambridge University Press, 1993.

Roe, Sir Thomas, *The Embassy of Sir Thomas Roe to the Court of the Great Mogul 1615-1619*, ed. William Foster, London, 1899.

Shah Nawaz Khan and 'Abd al-Hayy, *Ma'athir al-'umara'*, tr. Henry Beveridge, rev. Baini Prasad, 2 vols., Bibliotheca Indica, Calcutta, 1941-52.

Sobranie vostochnykh rukopisei Akademii Nauk Uzbekskoi SSR, 11 vols. to date, Tashkent: Sharqshunoslik Instituti, 1952-85.

Storey, Charles, *Persian Literature: A Bio-Bibliographical Survey*, London: Luzac, 1927-.

Welch, S.C., Jr., *India, Art and Culture 1300-1900*, New York: Metropolitan Museum and Holt, Rinehart and Winston, 1985.

Wolpert, Stanley, *A New History of India*, 5th edition, New York and Oxford: Oxford University Press, 1997.

Index of Names

About the Translator

Richard C. Foltz is the author of *Mughal India and Central Asia*. He holds a Ph.D. in history and Middle Eastern studies from Harvard University, and has taught at Brown University and Gettysburg College. He has recently been appointed Visiting Assistant Professor in the Department of Religion, Columbia University.